RAB STATES

Map showing Arab States with the following data:

- **ROMANIA, BULGARIA, TURKEY, SOVIET UNION, AFGHANISTAN, IRAN** (surrounding regions)
- **SYRIA**: 185,680 Sq.Km., 4,550,000 Pop. — Damascus
- **LEBANON**: 10,400 Sq.Km., 1,750,000 Pop. — Beirut
- **IRAQ**: Area 438,446 Sq.Km., Pop. 8,262,000 — Baghdad
- **JORDAN**: 90,000 Kms., 1,500,000 Pop. — Amman
- **ISRAEL**: Jews — Israel Citizens 2,345,000; non-Jews 312,000; Others 900,000 — Jerusalem
- **KUWAIT**: 24,280 Sq.Km., 468,000 Pop.
- **EGYPT**: Area 938,000 Sq.Km., Population 30,000,000 — Cairo
- **SAUDI ARABIA**: Area 2,400,000 Sq.Kms., Population 6,000,000 — Riyadh
- **Abu Dhabi**: 94,618 Sq.Km., 1,500,000 Pop.
- **MUSCAT & OMAN**: Area 212,000 Sq.Km., Pop. 750,000
- **YEMEN**: Area 195,000 Sq.Km., Pop. 550,000 — San'a
- **S. YEMEN PEOPLE'S REPUBLIC**: 160,300 Sq.Km., 1,500,000 Pop. — Aden
- **SUDAN**: Area 2,506,800 Sq.Km., Population 13,500,000 — Khartoum
- **ETHIOPIA, SOMALIA, KENYA, UGANDA, CONGO** (surrounding regions)

CARTA, JERUSALEM

Scale: 500 — 1000 KM.

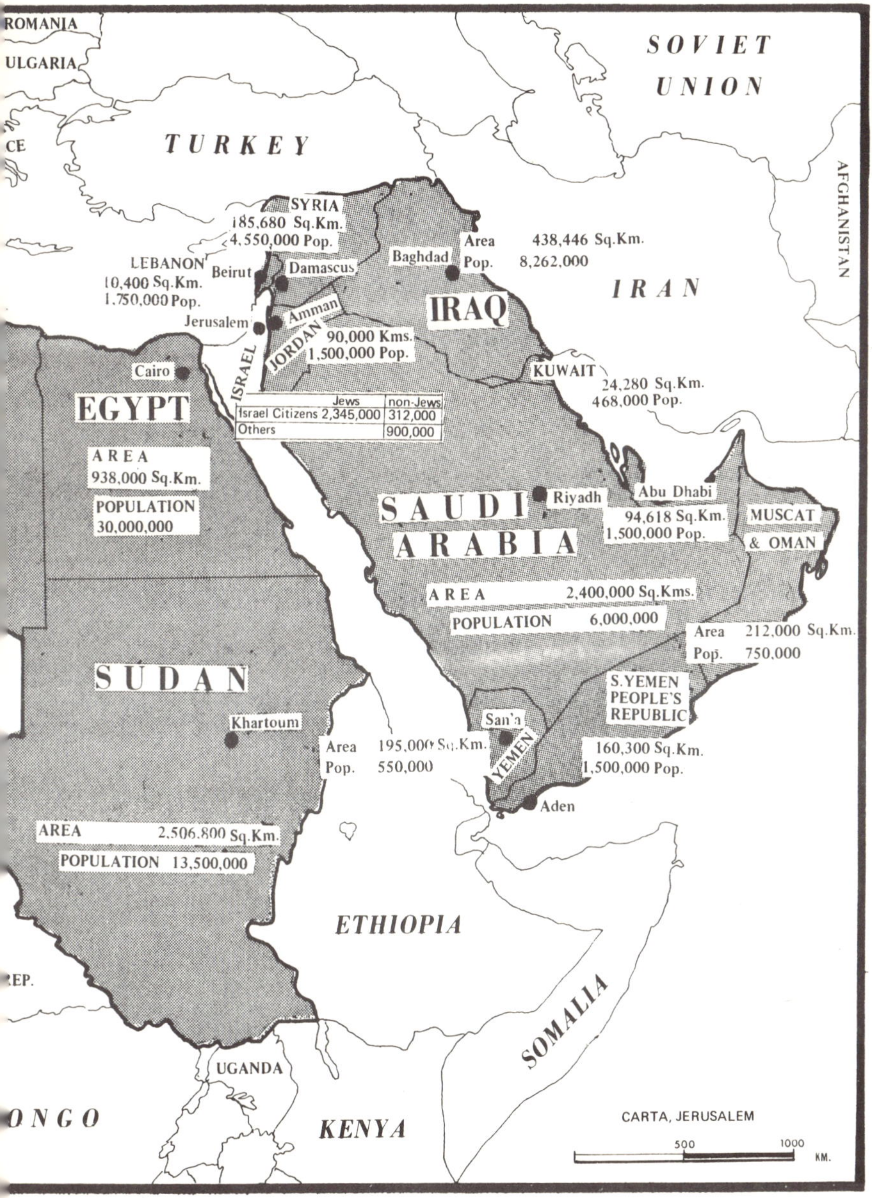

The Jewish Revolution
Jewish Statehood

THE JEWISH REVOLUTION

JEWISH STATEHOOD

by

ISRAEL ELDAD

Translated from Hebrew by Hannah Schmorak

A TIMES OF ISRAEL BOOK
SHENGOLD PUBLISHERS, INC.
New York City

Library of Congress Catalog Card Number: 79-163739
Copyright © 1971 by The Times of Israel
Published by Shengold Publishers, Inc.
45 W. 45th St., New York, N.Y. 10036
All rights reserved
Printed in the United States of America

To my son Aryeh

We are the rungs of a ladder, we are the links to the future;
This broadens our vision, yet restricts us;
This is a source of pride and a reason for modesty —
  May we be worthy of our role.

I. E.

JERUSALEM, 1971.

CONTENTS

1	An Existence of Non-Conformity	9
2	The Fall of the Bastille	17
3	Sources of Zionism—Two Old and One New	23
4	New Zionism Vs. The New Left or The Joseph Complex	31
5	Zionism as Liberation, Revolution and Renaissance	43
6	Right, Necessary and Possible	57
7	The Zionist Front in Soviet Russia	69
8	Intermezzo, Rhapsody, Caesura	79
9	*Eretz Israel* or Palestine	95
10	The Arab-Jewish Conflict	109
11	Before Any Court of Justice	121
12	Jordan Is a River, Not a State	129
13	Israel and Ismael	137
14	Three Points of No Return and Three Stages of Salvation	165
15	Israel	175

"TIMES OF ISRAEL" COVER REPRODUCTIONS

1

AN EXISTENCE OF NON-CONFORMITY

An essential non-conformity is the primary characteristic of the Jewish people. The large number of Jews who take part in various protest movements is easily explicable against the background of Jewish history. As long as the Jews are living amongst their own people, their non-conformist streak finds its satisfaction in the collective non-conformity of the Jewish existence, as compared with the life of other nations. In isolation, the Jew first tends to become ultra-conformist, in reaction to his former non-conformism when he was still sharing in the customs of his people. He tries as fast and thoroughly as possible to assimilate into his environment— Christian, liberal or national—so that he may no longer stand out from the rest. Many have tried this course of merging into the multitude. While they personally may have failed, their descendants, usually after three or four generations, finally achieved total immersion. Yet as a rule the experiment does not work.

Generally, despite all their efforts, gentile society continues to regard them as Jews. In the first assimilation movement on record, the Hellenization movement which was an attempt to adapt to the then dominant Helleno-Graeic culture, those ardent assimilationists who were trying to hide the marks of circumcision during the athletic events at which nudity was the rule were referred to as "stretching their prepuce." This stretching of the prepuce became a symbol of the ridiculous attempts of these Jews to assimilate to a foreign environment. For a long time the outstanding physiognomic characteristic of the Jew—his long, bent nose—was looked upon as a kind of symbolic displacement, the extension of one organ in compensation for the artificial shortening of another. Significantly enough, it was the long nose of the assimilated Jew that figured most prominently in anti-Semitic caricatures. For the Jew who remained Jewish there were plenty of other marks of recognition connected with his religion—his beard, his sidelocks or his dress. It is doubtful whether the recent nose-bobbing fashion would have been of much help to the assimilated Jews of those days. A nose modified by plastic surgery is not an inherent trait.

Gentile society never placed any reliance on assimilated or baptised Jews. Strangely enough, their distrust stemmed from the unconscious respect they had for the true Jew. Baptism or assimilation—they obscurely felt—were merely a ruse for infiltrating gentile society and vanquishing it through internal subversion. Others, conceding the latent strength and truth of Judaism, found it difficult to grasp why any Jew should escape from this bastion. When Dr. Max Nordau, Herzl's closest political ally said that a baptised Jew was not an honest man, he provoked an enormous outcry, yet he spoke nothing but the truth. There were very few indeed who had converted because of a sincere belief in Christian dogma. It was a home-truth that sooner or later had to be told.

There is the story of a Jewish socialist leader who had managed to escape from Germany during the Nazi regime, and found his way to England. At a reception held in his honour by the Labour party, the chairman welcomed him also as a Jew, but the staunch socialist waived this distinction by saying that he had left the Jewish community some time in the twenties. "I did not know Judaism was a kind of club," was the chairman's response.

There was another reason why the attempt to escape from the shackles of Judaism by means of outward conformity was doomed to failure. The Jew never managed to hide his peculiar talents. For there can be no doubt that in certain areas, especially in the intellectual field, the Jew has been endowed with special gifts and inclinations. Not only did he not hide his light under a bushel, but he did his best to boast of his talents, one of the main reasons for having abandoned the Jewish community having been the desire to be able to give them free rein. Soon, however, his special aptitudes were to betray him by swiftly pushing him to the top, where the gentiles, partly from envy and partly from mistrust, right away latched on to his Jewishness—either in a gross and direct fashion, especially in Eastern Europe, or with a biting subtlety, carefully preserving all the proprieties, as is the custom of the English-speaking countries.

The third way in which assimilation failed was through the emergence of individual nonconformism. The inherently rebellious character of the Jew tended to become still more pronounced with the disintegration of the collective or the detachment of the individual from the collective. It is no accident that Freud, the emancipated Jew, in his exploratory voyage into the depths of the human psyche did not go beyond the shores of the individual, while his gentile disciple Jung, deprived of the internal motivation to stop there, delved further into the chasms of the collective soul.

This non-conformist tendency, whether directed solely against the Jewish father image or against contemporary society as a whole, is the psychological impulse that has caused so many Jews, in the past and in the present, to take part in a variety of revolutionary movements. Evidently these movements were of the Leftist brand; first, because Jews were as a rule, though not always, debarred from the Rightist, frequently anti-Jewish movements; and secondly, because for a long time the left was swathed in an aura of social justice and thus exerted a preternatural attraction on the descendants of the ancient prophets and the recent victims of the existing regimes. The proportion of Jews in the ranks of the old as well as the new Left, as theoreticians and men of action alike, many of them endowed with an uncommon capacity for personal sacrifice deriving in no small measure from the tradition of Jewish martyrdom, is much higher than their percentage of the total population. This again is due to the same nonconformist streak that is a predominant characteristic of the Jewish people. In former ages, while they were still living in the ghetto this trait had helped the Jews to shape their autonomous existence and survive as a separate nation.

The nonconformity of the Jewish collective, or the revolutionary character of the Jewish people, found its expression in all three stages of its existence—its prehistoric evolution or national mythology, the period of statehood that lasted some thousand years, and the two thousand years of exile.

The term "mythology" when applied to the ancestral tales of the Jewish nation, the story of Abraham, for instance, is somewhat of a misnomer. Ordinarily, national mythologies consist of biographies of gods and demi-gods, men of divine origin or men who have turned into gods. Not so the story of the evolution of the Jewish people, whose main theme is a constant revolt against mythology. The term can be applied only insofar as it is taken to denote the pithy depiction of ancient figures that have come to embody an ideal and have been preserved in the consciousness of a people as a lasting legendary force, transcending mere historical fact.

A basic image of this kind in the consciousness of the Jewish nation is the figure of the patriarch Abraham. We are not so much concerned with the fact that critical scholarship has recently veered back to the view that Abraham was truly a historical figure, as with the artistic-psychological-educational aspect of his image as implanted in the heart of the Jewish nation, which has its origins not only in the Bible but even more so in story and legend. Abraham was the father of the Monotheistic revolution, the greatest of all rebels against the establishment, rising up against his own idol-worshipping father. Legend has it that he went so far as to smash all the idols on display in his father's pagan department store. He was a rebel who resorted to violence, and for his crime was sentenced by the tyrant Nimrod, the head of the all-powerful establishment, to death in a burning furnace . . . from which he came out alive. On the altar of his new-found faith he is willing to sacrifice his son—a much more difficult ordeal than sacrificing his own life. What is more, in the name of this faith in a single God, the God of justice and law, he is willing to stand up to that very Godhead: "Shall not the Judge of all the earth do right?" (Gen. 18, 25) says he in a violent argument about the imminent destruction of Sodom. This attitude of protest against a God in whom one yet never ceases to believe is a recurrent motif in Historical Books of the Bible, the Prophets and the Book of Job. It is an attitude that is completely at variance with the total submission demanded by all other religions, where such personal revolt, such claims and accusations against the Deity are quite inconceivable.

Recent historical research has shown that Ur Kasdim, the birthplace of Abraham, was a land of flourishing culture. And again the very words of the Bible, when Abraham *hears* the voice of God saying unto him: "Get thee out of thy country, and from thy kindred, and from thy father's house, unto a land that I will show thee," resound the call of revolt. Abraham is exorted to break all his ties with the past on his way to something new and unprecedented; to break not the ties of slavery, but the ties of gold that hold him to a prosperous land and home, and the ties of blood. But this is no anarchistic, nihilistic breakaway out of despair. It is a deliberate dissociation from a multitude of false gods, leading to a positive, new spiritual and intellectual experience, the experience of a single invisible God that has neither picture nor image. At the beginning of the second millennium B.C. when Abraham is presumed to have flourished, this concept of Divinity must have appeared both odd and strange, and it continued to be so throughout the subsequent two thousand years.

Then came the age of statehood, another period of mental and spiritual trial. The temptations to become "like unto the nations all around" were considerable. Here was a nation trying to go about its daily life in its own special way, in the midst of other, major cultures great in matter and in spirit; first, Egypt and Babylon, and then Greece and Rome. Moreover, it was not living in a remote corner of the world where it could set itself up against outside influence, but right on the crossroads between Asia, Africa and Europe—a highly delicate geopolitical position. Obviously the dangers and temptations to integrate within these major cultures to the point of total fusion and disappearance were enormous. Nevertheless the Jews managed to live the life of a normal nation, while at the same time preserving those spiritual, ethical and religious features that set them apart from all the rest. Prophecy and the *halakha* (the body of Jewish law evolved from the Bible through rabbinical exegesis) became the basis of individual and collective, constitutional existence. They set the rules that governed both private and public affairs. The fundamental monotheistic faith and the moral convictions with which these rules were imbued, and the Jews' supreme trust in God and in their own destiny, consistently helped them to preserve their national independence against the repeated onslaught of powerful empires and the seductions of more esthetic and hedonistic cultures, such as the Greek. These recurrent clashes were not without conflict. They provoked many a costly fight. But in the end the Jewish nation always emerged triumphant. It always managed to preserve its own existence and continue steadfast in its own way. Other nations, the major powers of those days, failed to understand this special quality of the Jews, their unbending urge to survive and retain their distinction. Yet the spirit of national existence, of Jewish statehood, managed to overcome even such major disasters as the destruction of the First Temple, the internal dissensions by which the people were rent, and the impact of Hellenism that swept the entire Middle East. The Jewish nation remained a non-conformist entity despite the surrounding welter and the drive to uniformity.

Afterwards came the end of territorial sovereignty. The nation was dispersed the world over. Two mighty religions —Christianity and then Islam—were swallowing up continents and nations. But not the Jews. They remained a separate enclave in this alien world. Times were hard. The temptations, too, were many. Ostensibly the monotheistic faith had won a tremendous victory. Why, then, should the Jews not give up their stubborn separatism and merge into the no longer pagan establishment—the Christian or the Moslem?

We are not concerned with theological matters and the differences between the Jewish faith and its two rivals. Our concern is with the survival of the Jewish nation, though deprived of its land and political sovereignty. For the Jewish people nevertheless managed to retain its autonomous existence. It did so without external compulsion but by an act of choice, by the exercise of its sovereign will to stand fast against a hostile environment that was alternately using seduction and oppression, the carrot and the stick, to win it over to its ways—or stamp it out.

This autonomous existence, moreover, was no mere vegetation. The Jews continued to live a full and independent life according to their own specific code—a life of constructive creation in the arts and the sciences. Their obstinate adherence to their own culture and their urge to survive caused no little amazement. Their unprecedented personal devotion, their willingness to make every sacrifice and undergo any martyrdom, coupled with their inalienable trust in their final redemption frequently aroused a sense of awe and fear in an uncomprehending environment. The miracle of their survival defied conventional history, and to this day continues to irk philosophers who are unable to fit this phenomenon into their world picture.

Neither Augustine nor Marx nor Toynbee was able to explain it according to their norms. Toynbee's anger at the Jewish nation's refusal to be neatly classified into any of his categories, the unanswerable challenge it presents to his theories, has caused him to declare that the Jewish nation is no more than a historical fossil. For him this may be a satisfactory way of dealing with what is to him merely a theoretical problem. It is not satisfactory for us, nor is it compatible with the simple fact of the existence of a living Jewish nation. Ironically enough, at about the same time as Toynbee arrived at his peculiar logical definition, that very "fossil" was in a very unfossil-like way fusilating the British from Palestine.

Also on the non-metaphysical, purely existential plane, the non-fossilised nature of the Jewish people is making itself manifest. It is manifesting itself in its struggles and efforts to create for itself a new sovereign existence in defiance of all historical "laws" and historiosophic logic—and of the will of many powerful nations.

Like the core figure of Abraham, which is essentially revolutionary in its history, legend and ideals, so has been the dynamic existence of the Jewish nation both during its period of territorial sovereignty and in the subsequent age of ex-territorial survival. Non-conformism was the hallmark of the Jewish people throughout. What is more, it was to this non-conformism that the Jews owed their survival as a living, creative and constructive people. It is quite sufficient to accept this basic trait as a fact without trying to look for abstruse explanations. Reasons will not alter the fact.

2
THE FALL OF THE BASTILLE

THE day the Bastille fell, the foundations were laid for the gas ovens of Auschwitz—and for the revival of the State of Israel.

This paradox does not only help us to understand the past, but also what is going on at present and is likely to happen in the near future among the Jews of the U.S.S.R. and the U.S.A.—the two classical diasporas that have remained after the establishment of the State of Israel.

And what is so paradoxical about this statement? The paradox is that the French Revolution, in its theoretical assumptions and reformatory zeal, was designed to ensure full civil liberties and equal rights for all and sundry. "Liberty, fraternity and equality" was its motto. Its projected outcome certainly did not include genocide as an outcrop of the abolition of religious and racial discrimination, nor was it a likely progenitor for the establishment of a Jewish state. Application of its tenets to the Jews could have been reasonably expected to lead to complete assimilation or at most, after the absolute separation between church and state had been accomplished, to their continued existence as one of several religious sects. Predictably, the Jewish question would have been practically solved.

Would have been—but in line with the essential paradox of Jewish existence, the Jewish problem failed to be solved with the emancipation. On the contrary, it was the emancipation that was to create what has since been referred to as the "Jewish Problem." Before the emancipation, before the Jews attained their civil liberties, there was no "Jewish problem." The Jews had their troubles and their difficulties, but Jewishness and Judaism constituted no problem. Their situation became problematic only when the walls of the ghetto came down and they were *formally* integrated in the cultural, social and political life of the various countries they happened to be in. Before the French Revolution no one ever dreamt of posing such questions as Napoleon put to the Jewish delegates to his Grand Consistoire, ironically referred to as the "Sanhedrin," the synod of seventy Jewish sages that during the period of statehood had laid down the law for the community. "Who are you?" he asked, "Jews or Frenchmen? What is your attitude to intermarriage? And if you keep praying for your salvation in Zion and Jerusalem, what is it you want from France? What will happen when war breaks out between France and England? Will you be willing to fight the Jews there?" These are but a few of the embarrassing and tragic dilemmas of double loyalty, hinging upon the schizophrenia inherent in the peculiar situation of the Jewish people.

It might be worthwhile mentioning at this point that during his Middle East campaign, before he had seized the reins of the French Government, and before he put these drastic questions to the Jews and revoked a considerable portion of the civil liberties granted to them by the Revolution, this same Napoleon had approached them with a view to establishing a Jewish state in Palestine. This was his first, momentary flash of genius, not unconnected with imperialist considerations. Then came the second alternative—complete assimilation. What he could not tolerate (and rightly so) was the limbo of uncertainty, the Jews being neither here nor there.

The theory of racial anti-Semitism was formulated not in Tsarist Russia with its millions of Jews, where not a decade passed without a pogrom or a ritual libel charge, but in Germany, where only one per cent of the population was Jewish and most of the Jews were assimilated or on the road to assimilation, and where the Jewish ghetto was almost a thing of the past. It was there that the idea was first conceived that Europe must be cleansed of its Jews. Afterwards, the only controversy was how this cleansing should be accomplished.

We have all heard of the Inquisition, but very few know that the Catholic Inquisition never persecuted loyal Jews. Its sole victims were the "marranos"—"pigs" in Spanish—who had converted to Christianity but were suspected of not being faithful to their new religion. Not that the Jews had an easy time of it—they suffered from numerous restrictions and repeated expulsions. It was, however, not until mass baptisms became the fashion that the Church grew alarmed lest the Jews were about to infiltrate into, and in this way take over, the Christian world.

With the fall of the French Bastille, the walls of the Jewish bastille also began to tumble. Large numbers of Jews left the ghetto and abandoned their former collective, national-religious way of life—some of them without any immediate desire to assimilate, others in a conscious urge to leave all that is peculiarly Jewish behind them. There were Jews who looked upon the emancipation, the conferment of legal equality and the catchwords of the Revolution as the veritable harbingers of salvation. Indeed, the worst pessimist could hardly have imagined that one hundred years after the French National Convention made its declaration of equal rights for the Jews, the Paris mob would scream "Death to the Jewish Traitors," as it did during the Dreyfuss trial when a French captain of assimilated Jewish parentage was falsely accused of treason. Nor could he have envisaged that a hundred years after Lessing wrote his *Nathan the Wise,* an ultra-liberal emancipationist work imbued with the pathos of justice and equality that appeared in Germany in

1779, the first official Anti-Semitic Congress should be convened in that country to demand the total ouster of the Jews, as a foreign and harmful element in German society. Had it not been for the emancipation, Jews would still have been hated and persecuted as before, but the racist Nazi theory would never have come into being nor would anyone have thought of "solving the problem" by utter physical annihilation.

This became possible after the external barriers had fallen, and to a large extent because they had fallen, and Jews had infiltrated into non-Jewish society not modestly and quietly, by the back door, but openly and visibly, swiftly rising to the top.

The paradox becomes still more striking when it is borne in mind that democracy not only failed to prevent this development but actually helped to promote it. In non-democratic times individual rulers could still decide the fate of "their" Jews, sometimes improving their conditions out of personal, humanitarian motives, or for reasons of material gain. When the masses became the supreme arbiters, religious, economic and social envy and hate all combined in times of crisis to foment anti-Semitic outbreaks, and through the democratic process found expression in the laws of the country, reflecting the will of the people. Pleas for mercy, bribes and other forms of intervention might have an effect on the former feudal rulers—nobles, kings and even bishops. All these were of no avail against an excited mob, looking for a scapegoat to blame for its own troubles. Under these circumstances the Jew was an easy prey. He could always be condemned, whether it be as a bloodsucking capitalist or a revolutionary communist, as a blaspheming atheist or a reactionary religious fanatic, as an exclusive particularist or a sneaking intruder trying to contaminate society by his blood or his spirit, as a nationalist or a cosmopolitan.

From Western Europe the ideas of the French Revolution spread to the East, but before the Jews of Russia had attained their first civil liberties, extreme racist anti-Semitic slogans were already resounding in the streets of Germany and France.

And that is what we meant by saying that the day the Bastille fell, the gas furnaces of Auschwitz were beginning to go up. Without emancipation and integration, either by way of assimilation or after the less drastic fashion of what is nowadays called acculturisation, the desire to bring about the ultimate annihilation of the Jews would never have arisen. Had they not attained to the position they did in gentile society, no plans to destroy them would have been hatched and certainly genocide would not have been attempted.

During the first stages of the French Revolution the Jews—with the exception of the ultra-orthodox—were among its most enthusiastic supporters. They composed such anthems as "France is our Zion, Paris our Jerusalem and the Seine our Jordan." The silver crowns of prayer shawls and golden ritual vessels from the synagogues were offered in Robespierre's "Temple of Reason." Torah scrolls were used to cover the drums beaten during the numerous liberty parades. Some hundred and fifty years later they came to be used for similar purposes, as drums and for boot leather—this time in Auschwitz.

For had the Bastille remained intact, there would have been no Auschwitz.

Nor would there have been modern Zionism to lead the Jews back to their own land.

3

SOURCES OF ZIONISM— TWO OLD AND ONE NEW

THE river Jordan, dividing the Land of Israel into two, rejoins both halves into one. Despite the shortness of its course, it is one of the most dynamic rivers in the world, descending some 3000 ft. over a stretch of only 300 miles. Hence its vigour and its numerous meanderings. At times it disappears from view, at others it is engulfed in a muddy swamp or in the lovely waters of Lake Galilee, to emerge again, intact and unharmed, like the nation that calls it its own.

The Jordan has three sources. Two are already in our hands. The third, the Hasbani, not yet. It is a misfortune rivers sometimes fall heir to. However that may be, it is up to us to use all these sources, so that none of the waters may be wasted or diverted by others.

* * * * *

Zionism, too, stems from two main sources, one positive and one negative.

The positive source is the incessant striving of the Jewish people for its own redemption, ever since the destruction of the Temple and the beginning of the exile. According to an ancient legend the Messiah was born on the day the Temple was destroyed—the Messiah being the figure that redeems the Jewish people from the diaspora, restores it to sovereignty in its own land, rebuilds the temple, enforces the law of the Torah—the law of justice and equity. All these are the essential preconditions of peace. The belief in ultimate salvation found expression in thrice-daily prayers and in a life built on a multitude of customs designed to keep this idea alive in the mind of the people, and remind them that their existence in the diaspora was only a temporary experience. It also gave rise to repeated Messianic movements—practical attempts to bring about the hoped-for salvation by concrete means. No other people has given evidence of such tenacious loyalty to its homeland after having lost physical contact with it. With the ordinary emigrant the memory of the "old home" begins to fade within two or three generations, and if a family happens to be particularly careful to preserve that memory, its pride of origin still remains without practical effect. Hence, until the period of emancipation, no one spoke about the Jews having *emigrated.* The Jews were in *exile,* moving from one diaspora to another until they might be redeemed and gathered in from the lands of their dispersion. A profound sense of exile was the foundation of their individual and collective consciousness. The early ghetto, of the pre-Nazi variety, was set up more out of the Jews' own volition than through outside coercion. The famous badge of shame the mediaeval Jew was required to wear in certain countries was never regarded as such by the Jews themselves. It was only when the emancipation did away with this and all other outward signs of Jewishness, that the first ingredients of shame and self-contempt entered the soul of the emancipated Jews. It was they who were the first to abandon the ideal of national salvation and to strike out all mention of Zion and Jerusalem from their prayerbooks so as not to be suspected of double loyalty.

 On the whole, however, the belief in Zion as the Jewish homeland was never abandoned. How to get back to that land—that was the question, and here opinions were divided.

Some tried to find their way back through mystical practices. Others attempted semi-political means to bring about a return. There also were, throughout the ages, small groups of pilgrims who made the long and dangerous trek to the Land of Israel. Of course there were also non-Jews who tried to keep up some ties with this country—Palestine as it was called since the Roman destruction—but these were limited to certain religious sites. The Land of Israel had never been their patrimony and was never regarded as such. Their affiliation with it was neither territorial nor political. The Jews outside the Land of Israel had more of a proprietary sense of belonging and an attachment to the land than any of the Christians and Moslems who happened to live in it. Even those Jews who made the long pilgrimage in order to *die* and be buried there, thought of it primarily as the land that held out the prospects of a better future for their people, a land of *life* and of hope; they did not merely cling to past memories, and ancient, religious myths. Among no other nation in the world have the memories of a distant past lived on so dynamically, as an essential part of the present and a binding pledge for the future.

This intrinsic, positive source, though of primary importance for the survival of the Jewish people and for the perpetuation of its faith in ultimate redemption through the retrieval of its homeland, by itself was not enough to secure that end. Another current had to be infused into the stream so that its flow might be strong enough to sweep the Jews along to their promised salvation. A positive idea, however great and beautiful and just, is not enough to provide the necessary motive force for a major, national undertaking. Individuals may be impelled by an idea alone. Masses also need a further impetus, a driving, compulsive force that pushes and coerces them.

Modern anti-Semitism provided the second, negative source for the rise of Zionism. For the believing Jew whose Jewishness was an act of will and choice and who was thus imbued with a sense of exile, redemption was a natural corollary of this state. The emancipated Jews who had lost this sense of exile first had to experience the bankruptcy of their own emancipation before they could espouse the Zionist ideal.

Shabtai Zvi in the 17th century was the last to try and bring about redemption by mystical-messianic means. The impact of his failure, greater than that of his many predecessors because his followers were more numerous, was such as to discourage the growing trend towards mysticism. It was a resounding smack in the face that the nation seemed to need in order to bring it back to reality, and prevent it from losing itself in abstruse speculations. In the same way the attempt to defect from the ranks of Judaism, to escape the common lot of the Jewish people through the cracks in the wall that opened with the fall of the Bastille, seemed to have been a necessary historical experience to demonstrate that such escape is impossible. Not only is it *not worth while* to dissociate oneself from the fate of this great nation that still has a great future before it, but it is also *impossible.*

For one's own self-respect it is no doubt better if one comes round to the Zionist idea of one's own free will, but there is nothing wrong with ending up in the right place by a more devious route, through the impact of the negative forces of external compulsion; as long, of course, as one does not get there too late, for the more devious route may also include the horrible alternatives of Auschwitz—or Siberia. (The corresponding place name for America is still unknown, but potentially the place exists, and in the present reality of the U.S.A. no one with a sound instinct of survival or critical sense will deny that potentiality.)

In another way, too, the emancipation that came after the fall of the Bastille filled an important function in the subsequent attainment of renewed statehood. Through it the Jews acquired the necessary modern know-how on a political level to be able to shoulder such an undertaking. To quote Herzl's retort when someone threw in his face that Shabtai Zvi already tried to save the Jewish people and failed: "But in our days there are trains and machines." Trains and machines and all the wonders of modern technology also did the work of the devil in the attempted extermination of the Jews. Towards the end of the nineteenth century, a hundred years after the fall of the French Bastille and the initial crumbling of the Jewish Bastille, a terrible race began between Satan and the Redeemer. There began the race between Nazism, which was, as stated, merely the executive agent of the immanent desire to get rid of the Jews by whatever means, fair or foul, and Zionism, which though largely fuelled by the forces of anti-Semitism, was again merely the executive agent of the immanent desire of the Jews to survive and be saved.

When the gates of the ghetto came down and ex-territorial Jewish autonomy became a thing of the past; when the twofold dangers of conversion and destruction threatened to put an end to the existence of the Jewish people in the diaspora, then salvation became a matter of urgent necessity, at last made possible by the advances of modern science and technology. It was no accident that most of the Zionist leaders who devised the tools for the implementation of Zionism and formulated its political thoughts were the products of the emancipation. With the exception of a few 19th century rabbis who derived their Return to Zion philosophy from the innate Jewish source, most of the religious leadership remained aloof from or hostile to political Zionism. There were those who clung to the mystical Messianic ideas. Others were motivated by not altogether groundless fears that this might be but another Shabtaic movement that would lead to new disappointments and a new wave of conversions; for had not Shabtai Zvi himself gone over to Islam, and his follower, Joseph Frank, to Christianity? That the harbingers of the Messiah should be men who fail to keep the Sabbath and the ritual laws of purity was unacceptable to the religious leaders. In vain Herzl courted the rabbis of his time to convince them to take part in the establishment of a new mass movement that would stage a modern exodus. Yet he managed to enlist the masses over the heads of their religious leaders.

Not that the original messianic yearnings were alien to him, but he himself also first had to be hit in the face in order to grasp the true contemporary situation of the Jews. The enlightening shock came when, as a journalist, he was sent out to cover the trial of that French officer of Jewish extraction, Captain Dreyfuss whom we have already mentioned, who was falsely accused of treason and whose sentence and demotion caused the Paris mob to break out in cries of "Death to the Jews." It was in the same city that a hundred years before had dawned the light of human equality, the end of all religious and racial hate and discrimination. Herzl on this occasion learned what many have not yet learned from the extermination of six million Jews. He saw there what not everybody was able to discern in Auschwitz.

It is not surprising, therefore, that at times he felt like a modern Moses; for Moses, too, had grown up in the House of Pharaoh, and he too had his eyes opened by what appeared to be individual chance—by witnessing an Egyptian beating one of his Hebrew brethren.

Religious Judaism, steeped in its yearnings for salvation and in the belief in Messiah the son of David, expected the analogy to be carried through down to a new revelation in the burning bush and a magic staff that would perform signs and miracles. At the very least these Jews expected a Messiah who was himself an observant Jew, and they conceived of the new state along theocratic lines.

This Herzl failed to give them. His was a new language they did not know and understand. Hence the two sources, the positive and the negative, initially failed to coalesce.

Although the masses were inspired by a new enthusiasm at Herzl's actions and ideas which responded both to their physical needs, especially in Eastern Europe, and to their innate love of Zion, religious orthodoxy at first refused to follow.

Herzl's idea that the plight of the Jews, the Jewish problem, anti-Semitism, would provide the fuel for his train of rescue to the Jewish State was perfectly correct. It was not his fault, nor the fault of his idea, that for one-third of the nation, for six million whose end he foresaw and tried to prevent, the Jewish state came too late. For reasons we shall not go into here, the Zionist movement after Herzl's time departed from the revolutionary course that he had set for it in the knowledge that there was not enough time to go slow, that it was necessary to run fast if the race was to be won.

In Europe the race between perdition and salvation that had started with the fall of the Bastille and the emergence from the ghetto was getting close to its finish towards the end of the 19th century. It reached its finish in the middle of the 20th century.

The establishment of the Jewish state succeeded the final extermination of the Jews of Europe by a very short space of time. An interval of only three years separates the two events (1945-1948). This is not the place to analyse the reasons for this tragic delay. It is enough to point to the close juxtaposition to realise that annihilation was not a historical imperative; the establishment of a Jewish state was. Herzl understood, Nordau understood, Jabotinsky understood. Others understood a little, or a little too late.

We saw fit to mention this tragic delay because the race is not yet over. The devil puts on different guises before he finally gives up. He must have derived considerable encouragement from the fact that there were people in Israel who thought that with the establishment of the State, Zionism had reached its goal: The Jews have a state of their own like all other nations. This state has its difficulties; it has its religious, economic and security problems. But it exists and there ends the vision. The devil certainly leaped at the chance, pouncing upon this fatal fallacy in order to try and make good his losses. Only the Six-Day War and the recent events in the U.S.S.R. have once again shaken Israel and world Jewry out of their lethargy, to show them that the State of Israel is only the bridge to salvation, a new instrument for its attainment. The Jewish problem continues to exist despite the fact that the Jews have a state of their own. For the Jewish state never was an end in itself. It was a means for rescuing the Jewish people from the threat of annihilation through conversion and destruction that began to loom large ever since the fall of the two Bastilles—the gentile and the Jewish. The State of Israel is merely the transformation of Zionism into a state setting, where it is immeasurably stronger and more effective than in the setting of a voluntary Zionist organization, rich in vision and poor in resources. All the resources at the disposal of the State of Israel will, however, be useless unless they are backed by the original vision of Zionism deriving from the mainspring of the ancient messianic urge for complete salvation, and the immediate need to rescue the body of the nation which remains, as before, exposed to tremendous dangers.

And here we come to the third source referred to in the title of this chapter. To the two sources that have combined to create the Jordan of Zionism—the inbuilt drive for salvation and external anti-Semitism—a third source has been added—the State of Israel. A strong, triumphant and not a weak-kneed, wavering, support-seeking State of Israel has become a third, revolutionary and revolutionising admixture to the current. The fruit of Zionism has turned into the seed of a new Zionism, especially—so far—in the U.S.S.R., where the great Jewish revolution has received an astonishing impetus which holds out much hope for the future.

4

NEW ZIONISM Vs. THE NEW LEFT OR THE JOSEPH COMPLEX

ON the 50th Anniversary of the Communist Revolution in Russia, *Pravda* devoted its leading article to a brief historical review. An editorial marking so important an event was, no doubt, carefully vetted by the Soviet elite. Stalin no longer being in power—though a Neo-Stalinist period might well be in the offing—the editors again saw fit to include the name of Leib Trotsky, Lenin's right- (or left-) hand man, the founder of the victorious Red Army. How? Not by rehabilitating the memory of a hero who was treacherously murdered by Stalin's henchmen but still—or once again—by denouncing him. What interests us here, however, is less the actual denunciation as the form that it took. The editors of *Pravda* chose to refer to Trotsky not as an imperialist lackey, a Nazi agent, a traitor or a fascist, nor even as a Titoist or a Maoist. *"Judash Trotsky"* was the epithet they chose.

Judash—the worst swearword of the Slavic-Christian, Catholic or Pravoslavic world, after that Judas Iscariot, who according to the New Testament betrayed Jesus for thirty pieces of silver, and whose name has become synonymous with traitor and informer the Christian world over. In Eastern Europe, where it was applied indiscriminately to any Jew, its pejorative meaning was still further enhanced by conveying the blanket implication that all Jews are informers, money-grubbers, men who betray God for the sake of mammon.

One has got used to the Soviet press referring to Jews as the agents of capitalism, and to Zionists as the agents of imperialism, even as the aiders and abettors of Nazism. But the use of the term *Judash* in the official organ of the Communist Party on the 50th anniversary of the Communist, rationalist, atheist revolution, makes one wonder. From what psychic depths was it dragged forth, and to whom is it supposed to appeal, whose emotions is it expected to stir up?

For fifty long years the Soviet regime has been waging an anti-religious educational campaign against all religions. For fifty years it has tried to eradicate the belief in Jesus Christ. And then it comes and rifles the stores of religious terminology; it turns to what Marxist-Communist philosophy considers the opiate of the people for its invective.

Jesus himself might be a mere figment of the imagination, the man who never was; but the Jew, Judas Iscariot, nevertheless bore false tales against him, sold him, betrayed him. . . .

And thus Leib—the Yiddish equivalent of Judah the lion-cub—Leib Trotsky is turned into *Judash,* the man who sold out the glorious revolution for thirty pieces of silver or thirty thousand dollars.

Only if one grasps the specific implication of this word and its appearance in the anniversary editorial of *Pravda* can one fully comprehend what is going on in the U.S.S.R. to-day. It is only then that one realises the depth of the tragedy represented by the waste of Jewish vigour and intellect that has been sacrificed on the altar of Marxism.

One of the most serious handicaps the Jewish people suffered in counteracting the annihilation decreed upon them towards the end of the 19th century by the doctrine of anti-Semitism was its infatuation with Socialism and Communism. Their liberalism had blamed the feudal and absolutist regimes—with their religious obscurantism—and to some extent also the Jews' own separatist tendencies for the all-pervasive hostility the Jews had to contend with. And then the liberalist ideal triumphed almost everywhere. The Jews were formally emancipated. But anti-Semitism, far from abating, flourished, was built up into a "scientific" theory on the one hand, and won increasing acclaim among the masses, on the other. Hence the progressive liberals certainly did not have the answer.

Marxism—the doctrine of the baptised Jew, Karl Marx, and his disciples—did, or pretended to have the solution. Anti-Semitism, it said, was the outcome of class distinctions, of capitalism and its reactionary regimes. True enough, the Jews themselves were among the founders and defenders of capitalism. According to the Marxist creed the God of the Jews was the god of mammon. However that may be, it was clear that the triumph of socialism, of the reformist, Fabian or the revolutionary brand, would put an end to this hate. The new regime would be based wholly on reason and the equality of the working man. Nationalism, too, was doomed to fade and disappear. The French Revolution merely set the scene for the true revolution that would lead to a world of genuine equality and justice.

The present flirtation of many Jewish youngsters with the New Left cannot hold a candle to the spell that the socialist-communist ideal cast over the young Jewish generation at that time. It is no exaggeration to say that the best Jewish minds, the nation's greatest mental and physical resources, were sacrificed on the altar of this new God. "The proletariat has no homeland!"—Could any slogan have appealed more to a generation of young, emancipated Jews who, as the descendants of a homeless nation, were deprived of the opportunity to assimilate *en masse*, as most of them would have liked to do? Here they were offered a new kind of emancipation, which calls for no national, territorial ties and does away with the last watered down vestiges of Jewish separatism, the confessional affiliation with the "Mosaic faith" still lingering in liberal circles. They were all the more eager to follow the call since the socialist ideal responded to the sense of equality and justice deeply imbued in the Jewish nation both through the heritage of its prophets and its accumulated resentment of oppression and discrimination. Moreover, Marxism as a scientific method, gave the sophisticated Jewish mind an opportunity to sharpen its wits not on the Talmud and on religious disputations, but on the more dignified disciplines of economics and sociology. Now at last the Jewish individual was able to leave his mental and physical ghetto to embrace human society at large—no longer by an act of grace for which he had to pay by conversion or by swearing allegiance to an alien nationality, but as a human being *per se,* a citizen of the world, shedding all masks of super-patriotism and super-loyalty.

If there was a war-like, non-conformist element in this course they espoused, if the ideal called for a willingness to mount the barricades, to languish in prison and to court death, all the better. Jewish youngsters certainly had the necessary enthusiasm and zeal: the same enthusiasm and zeal that had inspired Jews for many generations to court every form of martyrdom in the ardent conviction of the truth and justice of their faith.

So far no exact estimate has been made—and by now it may be too late—of how many Jewish lives have been offered to this Moloch, how many years have been wasted in prison, how much physical, mental and emotional energy went down this drain. It might be well worthwhile to sum up what this effort has cost the nation in leadership potential —for practically all the leaders, from Marx on, were Jewish; to tote up the price in terms of the active rank and file, down to those boys and girls who spent their best years in prison for distributing Communist propaganda, and those early pioneers in *Eretz Israel* who volunteered to take part in the Spanish civil war or go back to the U.S.S.R., only to be arrested and die in Siberia. There were countries in Eastern Europe where the words Communist and Jew became synonymous, with no little justification. Though it may be rather absurd to accuse a single people of two such contradictory crimes as ultra-capitalism and communist revolutionism, the Nazis were able to do so.

Strangely enough, it was among the lower classes that the Jewish Marxist trend gave rise to increased anti-Semitism. People resented the Jews trying to belittle their own national and religious values. More than once Theodore Herzl, in his talks with various heads of state, used the argument that only Zionism was likely to avert the danger of masses of Jewish youngsters and intellectuals joining revolutionary, anti-capitalist movements, and some cite this as one of the reasons for the Balfour Declaration.

Yet the scaled-down, evolutionary Zionism after Herzl's times was no match for the revolutionary charisma of Marxism. The Jewish socialist revolutionaries, in their desire to escape the Jewish fate, were convinced they had found the perfect prescription: euthanasia. The Jewish people was to be put out of its misery through idealistic motives, when there would no longer be any need for selfish, individual defection.

When we look back at what Zionism nevertheless managed to accomplish although it attracted only a minority of Jewish youngsters and intellectuals; when we consider the tremendous achievement of the State of Israel, which came into being in defiance of the laws of history, we can easily imagine how much more could have been done had all the resources that were wasted on revolutions the world over been concentrated on this single goal—the cause of Jewish liberation. We might by now have had a state extending "from the Euphrates to the River of Egypt," with some ten million Jews engaged in industry and the arts, in agriculture and the sciences. We could have established a tremendous bastion for the Jewish people, extending its beneficial influence far beyond its own boundaries. Above all, there is no doubt that we could and would have attained lasting peace for the entire Middle East. Yet so much of our military, scientific and economic genius, so much of our dynamic spirit and devotion have gone to waste, spent in ways useless and often harmful to ourselves.

The innumerable individual tragedies of revolutionary Jews who have experienced the same fate as Trotsky and Slansky, the myraids who were cast off after having been exploited to the limit, to be physically or mentally annihilated when the Red god failed, combine to form a major *national* tragedy. Had this potential been properly channeled the destruction of European Jewry could undoubtedly have been prevented, and our positive achievements would have been substantially greater. If all this had been only a matter of the past one could dismiss it as a passing aberration, and having drawn the moral to be learned from it, go on from there. But the Jewish people, despite its phenomenal historic memory for events that occurred in Egypt 3,500 years ago, yet again includes major sectors, especially among the young, who are repeating the same tragic mistake.

We have already spoken about the revolutionary, nonconformist figure of Abraham, the man who smashed his father's idols for the sake of a shining new faith. For a better insight into what is going on at present it might be worth while to delve into our collective memory for another ancient story that likewise has the force of a natural myth —the story of Joseph in Egypt. Joseph was sold into slavery and served his foreign masters loyally. Then a false charge was brought against him and he was thrown into prison, from where he emerged thanks to his own wits and talents to become the virtual ruler of Egypt. We may look upon him as the proto-Freud, because he devised a new method for interpreting dreams that the wise men of Egypt had never heard of. He also was the proto-Marx because he solved Egypt's economic problems—the famine that was ravaging the country—in truly socialist fashion, by nationalising the fields, the crops and the livestock so as to share out those resources equally, and tide the country over the period of emergency. But then, he may also be regarded as the archtype of the assimilated Jew; he married an Egyptian woman, changed the style of his clothes, cut off his beard, changed his name, took no interest in his father and his brothers in Canaan until they came to him—all according to the well-known pattern. He managed to shed everything—except his sense of justice as revealed in the regime he imposed on Egypt, and his wit and talents that elevated him from prison to the highest post in the kingdom. And it worked, until ". . . there arose up a new king over Egypt, which knew not Joseph." Joseph had done his job and could be dispensed with, and the persecution of the Jews of Egypt could begin.

This, in short, is the story of Joseph, and it also is the story of the Jewish people among the nations—in or outside the ghetto, in the role of the saviours and of the oppressed. It is they who give of their genius to the world—the genius of Moses and Jesus, of Spinoza and of Marx, of Freud and Einstein, of Disraeli and Trotsky, of Slansky and Oppenheimer and Teller and Heine and Bergson and Kafka and thousands of other descendants of Joseph. Until there arises a Hitler or a Stalin, often thanks to the Jews' own endeavours. Because ingratitude for their cultural contribution to the world has become a law of history. Not only that, but the more gratitude is owed to the Jews, the more they are hated, for no-one likes his benefactor, especially a benefactor who all too often serves as one's latent conscience. To this we may also partly attribute the profound hatred for the Jews that we have witnessed in Russia from the days of the blood libels down to the doctors' trials in Stalin's times and the cloud of hate that is descending upon that country today.

With one slight difference; that the charges levelled against the Jews of the U.S.S.R. at present are no longer false. Joseph was still naive, but all the many Josephs who have given their lives for the Revolution have in the meantime come to see their new Pharaoh in his true light. Instead of being imprisoned and killed on such trumped-up charges as plotting to poison the leaders of Russia or being the agents of Imperialism, Jewish intellectuals and youngsters in the U.S.S.R. of to-day prefer to answer a real charge: that they are Jews and Zionists who want a new, great exodus from the modern Red Egypt. If they are in any case doomed to prison, forced labour and Siberia, they might as well suffer in dignity, for the sake of the truth they believe in.

The revolution that is now taking place in the U.S.S.R., in which the Jews are finally getting rid of their Joseph complex, their compulsion to be the loyal slaves of others, stems not only from a new awareness of the ingratitude they have suffered, but also, and perhaps mainly, from the new vigour derived from a fighting, victorious State of Israel. But we shall leave that for later. First we shall review those areas where the Joseph complex still operates in its old, destructive way.

One of these is the New Left.

Psychologically the New Left is an understandable, and tragically enough, perhaps also a deep-seated, phenomenon. It sprang up against the background of many bitter disappointments; with a fossilised liberal establishment which rests on its laurels though having lost its ideals; with many social and world problems that have not been solved despite the advances of science and technology; and with the state of those countries where the Communist ideal is being implemented—their schisms and corruption and methods of terror and intimidation. Partly it is also inspired by the fear of possible future nuclear wars. Despite all these deep psychological motives, however, the New Left is neither as profound nor as well-founded as were the Socialist or Communist movements before it. Socialism and Communism had a much firmer theoretical, philosophical, economic and historical foundation. They also had a more realistic and systematic conception of the alternative that to their minds should be substituted for the existing regimes. In all these respects the New Left is very poor. It also lags behind its forerunners in political acumen and drive. The Marxist movements set up a huge apparatus, on trade union or party lines, to implement their programs either by way of reform or by way of revolution. The New Left has failed to do so, for reasons we need not go into here.

To this must be added a further element that diminishes the stature of the New Left and makes it less serious than the classical, old Left. The personal zeal of the older revolutionaries can hardly be compared with the feverish ardour of present-day lecturers, students and propagandists of the New Left, which expends itself in a few protest meetings and demonstrations, some acts of violence, sit-ins, sit-outs, and the occasional riot—all transitory and of no serious consequence. In another few years an interesting sociological survey may probably be made showing the high percentage of New Leftists who have dropped out on reaching a certain age or attaining a certain position in society. The liberal movements in the Communist countries, the Black revolution and the white backlash in the U.S.A. are much more significant and potentially dangerous than the New Left because their prospects of success are far greater.

Nevertheless a book dealing with the State of Israel as the manifestation of and the means for the great Jewish revolution cannot ignore this movement which quite unsurprisingly boasts a high proportion of Jews in its ranks—again several times higher than their percentage of the total population. There is nothing at all astonishing about this, because it is a mere reproduction of the same mechanism, the same age-old complex, the same response to a variety of social, and psychological, collective and individual factors, the same mixture of positive and negative elements. The positive elements consist of the moral fervour of this movement, its protest against the greed, the corruption and the discriminatory practices of so-called revolutionary regimes, and its revolt against the vicious circle of bloody wars to end all wars.

On the negative side, especially for Jews, is the renewed suicidal urge, the desire once again to cease to be Jewish, after all previous attempts in this direction have failed. This is all the more negative because it is also of necessity accompanied by manifestations of self-hate, projected in the adulation of a variety of movements which, though of a doubtful revolutionary nature have a definite anti-Jewish and anti-Israeli trend. Thus the New Left is on the side of those who denounce the Jews as landlords and shopkeepers, as being members of the upper middle classes and supporters of the establishment, as the backers of Israel the imperialist agent, the oppressors of the Arabs, and many more. And still on the red side of the ledger is the fact that this new idealism of Jewish youth is doomed to meet the same end as its many predecessors. After the Jewish brains have been picked dry and much Jewish blood has been shed—Jews have already given their lives for this cause—they will again be dismissed. If they do not want to leave of their own free will, they will be thrown to the dogs. Then the whites in South Africa will suddenly remember that the Jews were actively inciting the Negroes against them, and the Negroes of South Africa will remember that the Jews are members of the white race that has been exploiting them. The Negroes in America will remember that the Jews are the establishment, while the white backlash movement will cast the blame on both Marcusism and Marxism and will recall the names of Oppenheimer and the Rosenbergs. Teller's name will count for little among them, nor will Chomski's count for much among the blacks, in the same way as the memory of Trotsky fails to appeal to Podgorny today, and Henri Bergson's achievements were no protection against Lavalle, the French writer Selin, a communist turned Nazi.

Whoever has failed to note the clockworklike recurrence of this cycle has wilfully or unconsciously ignored the lessons of history. He knows nothing about the workings of society in general and of Jewish society in particular.

The prototype of this phenomenon, the story of Joseph, already contains one cyclic repetition. Joseph was the faithful servant of Potiphar, until Potiphar's wife came up with her false allegation and he was thrown into prison. Joseph still thought—as we may note by reading the story carefully —that this was merely an accident. He believed that he just happened to fall into the hands of an evil woman, whose husband, his master, was too naive to uncover her wiles. Consequently he repeated the same exercise once again, but this time on a larger scale. He preserved Pharaoh's throne and saved Egypt from famine and social inequality. He put all his wits at the disposal of this Pharaoh and as his prime minister served him with such loyalty that he did not go back to his father's home in Cana'an, but caused his father and brothers to come to Egypt and willingly assume their first exile.

Joseph did not live long enough to witness the inevitable reaction. The Egyptians had no gas chambers, but they did fairly well with forced labour camps, and the Nile to drown the children of Israel in.

Until the arrival of Moses. His story too, might have ended in another attempt to deploy Jewish talents in the service of others, for Moses had grown up in Pharaoh's household. And then, coming to the land of Goshen, "he spied an Egyptian smiting an Hebrew, one of his brethren." In disgust he might have set up a New Left Movement. He might have filed suit against the Egyptian. As one so close to the court he might have tried to reform the regime.

But no. Moses had his fill of Egypt, and he was going to take his people out of there. This is how he became the true saviour of his nation—not by making revolutions in Egypt, but by leading his people out of that country. Here was a man who did not get caught in the cycle.

And the same goes for us.

After the white emancipation came the red emancipation, and when this too failed, came Hitler and Stalin. By now we should have learned our lesson: to use all our resources only for our own purposes and not waste them on others. A child, once scalded, has learned a useful lesson. If it happens a second time he is a fool. But if he lets it happen a third time—he is a pathological case.

In the past one might still have found some reasons or excuses for wanting to get away from the ghetto (although in some respects the ghetto offered more freedom and a more cultured way of life than the world of Voltaire, Dostoevsky, and Wagner, three arch-anti-Semites). Today the ghetto no longer exists. Nor can there be any question of getting away from it. Today we have the same option before us as in Moses' times: the option of freedom, of a new, triumphant Zionism, the great Jewish Revolution in *Eretz Israel*.

5

ZIONISM AS LIBERATION, REVOLUTION AND RENAISSANCE

As this book is not intended as a history of Zionism, we shall not try to analyse the tragic question why Zionism experienced several decades of slow motion, when both immigration and settlement proceeded at a snail's pace contrary to the wish of its visionary founder, Dr. Herzl, and in spite of the clouds gathering over Europe. Was it due to objective conditions which prevented the implementation of the Return to Zion in a revolutionary manner, through a mass exodus similar to the Egyptian exodus of Moses' times? Or was it due to subjective reasons stemming from the paltry vision and insufficient daring of the Jewish leadership? Or to the various subsidiary objectives that Zionism also tried to accomplish along the way which weakened its impact, and diverted precious resources from the main effort of rescuing the Jewish people from the diaspora?

I have already hinted where the blame should be sought. Here suffice it to mention the tragic fact that for the six millions who were exterminated (a *third* of the whole nation) the State of Israel came at least ten years too late, although Herzl had foreseen their fate, and in the last nine feverish years of his life burned out his heart to save them.

On Mount Herzl in Jerusalem—its most meaningful historic site apart from the Temple Mount—stands Herzl's tomb, a big black stone which bears but the single word *Herzl*. When you stand there, facing the wonderful city of Jerusalem with its many valleys and hills, you have on your right the *Yad Vashem* Memorial commemorating the holocaust in Europe. There you will find file after file of Jewish communities that have been destroyed; lists of men and women and children drawn up with meticulous German precision to record their entry to Auschwitz; urns containing the ashes of those who were burned; and pieces of soap that were made from their flesh. There you will find ample written and pictorial evidence of the greatness of the nation that was destroyed and of the techniques by which this destruction was accomplished. In a small, symbolic memorial chamber you will stand and bow your head, not only with grief but also with guilt and shame. For it is a shame that so experienced and wise and great a nation, so often forewarned both by its enemies and its own prophets, should have let itself be surprised by events and not saved itself in good time.

But standing near Herzl's tomb facing the city of Jerusalem, you also have the military cemetery on your left with rows upon flowering rows commemorating the hundreds and thousands who have fought and fallen for the liberation of their country, in their own war of liberation. Your heart may fill with sadness at the loss of this brave youth, but you bear your head high. These deaths were worthwhile. In the *Yad Vashem* Memorial you intone the ancient prayer, "God who is merciful" for only God in heaven can show compassion and forgiveness for the events commemorated there. But here you stand and sing *Hatiqva*—the Zionist anthem of revival and hope.

An inscription at the entrance to *Yad Vashem* reads: *Remembering is the root of salvation, and exile is the outcome of forgetfulness.* These were the words of Israel Baal-Shem-Tov, the creator of the Hassidic movement.

All these things are there to tell you that Herzl's prophetic vision called for a Zionist revolution, and if we dawdled and delayed once, at least the course of history and the terrible price we have paid for our remissness should teach us—

That the State of Israel came too late for six million of our brethren, partly because so many thought "it cannot happen here," and partly because so many thought that there was time galore; and—

That the State of Israel never was and never can be an end in itself. It has many intrinsic values, which we shall still come to; but at present the supreme value of renewed Jewish statehood lies in its being the tool for the accomplishment of an act of redemption that is not complete as long as there still remains a diaspora.

Whoever says that the present diaspora, after the establishment of the State of Israel, is no longer a state of exile but simply the dispersion of Jews over different countries has learned nothing and forgotten everything—a forgetfulness that again becomes the root of exile, a new cause for disaster. More than semantic quibbling, it borders on an act of criminal irresponsibility and felonious folly. This kind of thinking is merely an ideological superstructure erected over a foundation of careless complaisance, heedless hedonism and establishmentarian expediency.

Anyone who once again says, at this date and age, that we can wait, that there is ample time, takes upon himself the responsibility not for his own life alone, but for those millions who may once again pay with theirs. Not only the Jews of the U.S.S.R. but the Jews of the whole world are living in exile, and however sweet the exile might seem, this does not detract from the fact that this is what it is. For Herzl, one Dreyfuss Affair was enough. He did not need the horrors of Auschwitz and the terrors of Russian Jewry to bring the truth home to him.

Zionism implies a total revolution, total and not totalitarian, though the transfer of millions can never be a luxury trip. No revolution is. Where conditions are first-class, no revolution is needed. Whenever it is a question of saving masses of people, from war—especially of the modern, non-chivalrous variety—from earthquakes or any other catastrophe, many non-essentials must be given up for the sake of the future. Many sacrifices are called for.

Zionism is a revolution and neither a philanthropic institution nor a reform movement. It is concerned with the shift of an entire nation from an exposed position to a place of refuge.

Anti-Semitism is no extinct volcano, not anywhere in the world. In some places it may not be belching fire yet but only emitting a thin jet of smoke. Only the most sensitive seismographs may as yet indicate its subterranean rumblings. But the volcano is alive and only fools and worse fail to heed it.

Already in the Bible it is written—"and among those nations ye shall find no rest." As long as the Jewish people is exiled from its own country, it can find no ultimate peace anywhere else. So much for the law of God.

As for those who do not believe in divine law, perhaps they might be convinced by a more down to earth kind of law—the endless repetition of historic events. Perhaps they may try to learn from what happened in every diaspora—in Babylon and Egypt, in Spain and in Poland and in Germany, in Christendom and Islam, in the lands of religious and anti-religious fanaticism, in kingdoms and republics. If he fails to discern any pattern, any historic law in any of these, he must be blind. As for those who are not willing to make deductive inferences from the anomaly of the Jewish people, from its tenacity and emotional strength, from the social, economic and cultural position it occupies among the nations and by which it woos their hate and envy, perhaps they might be willing to approach the problem inductively, by adding one incident and one statistical fact to the other: Summing up all the various items they encounter in the street, the office and the factory, the radio and the press will they not be forced to conclude that a renewed wave of hatred and persecution, deportation and slaughter, though perhaps not inevitable, is at least probable or possible. And if so, is the very possibility as such not enough?

Why again wait until it is too late and there is no option left?

After the First World War, Max Nordau, the first prominent figure to join Herzl, suggested the mass transfer of hundreds of thousands of Jews to *Eretz Israel*. That was before the British had begun to restrict immigration. His opponents, the evolutionary Zionists, argued that it could not be done for economic reasons, for what would these masses be fed on? And Max Nordau, a scientist and a man of the rational, evolutionary 19th century, replied: Even if sixty thousand should starve, it would still be worthwhile.

Does anybody object on humanitarian grounds? His was the most humanitarian suggestion possible. And it was not humanitarianism but expediency, convenience, complacency, weakness of character and miscalculation that prompted Herzl's followers to adopt the course of slow, selective Zionism. The result was not that 60,000 starved, but that six million died in Auschwitz.

Zionism as a revolution has no peer and equal. The Russian Communist revolution and the Chinese Communist revolution certainly did not lack in greatness, as must be admitted even by those who have their doubts about the utopia they were aspiring to. What is now going on in Africa —a leap from a primitive tribal structure to the era of the modern national state—certainly represents a great revolution. Many borders will probably still be moved and many tribes annihilated before the new social and political structures come into being.

But all these were revolutions made by people living in their own territory. It was the jungle of their own land or human landscape which they turned over and reploughed to change their agrarian systems, their economic patterns, their class structure.

The Jewish revolution, besides all these, has several further tasks to accomplish. It must transfer a nation of millions from dozens of lands of dispersion to one single country. This it must do against the wishes of many of these lands and of the residents of *Eretz Israel* and its neighbours, and sometimes even against the wishes of the Jews themselves or at any rate without their conscious, immediate, absolute and unconditional consent. Every Jew, or practically every Jew, makes his own conditions for his salvation; only with or without a yarmulke; or only with a yarmulke of a specific size; only under a socialist regime or a regime of free capitalist enterprise; only at the highest standard of living or without any bureaucratic or other involvements. If you offer him the paradise he wants, readymade, then perhaps, maybe, if it should become really necessary, and provided that . . .

Until there comes the time when he is locked up in a ghetto or behind barbed wire or an iron curtain. Then he no longer makes conditions but runs to whatever border he can find.

In addition, the Jewish revolution has the task of welding the Jews from all the different diasporas together and giving them one single language. The revival of Hebrew as a vernacular, as the language used in industries and offices, in the army and in the university, in the marketplace and on the schoolbench, constitutes a revolution by itself, the magnitude of which has been realized by only a few. In a way it stands for all that has been accomplished in many other fields as well.

From ancient, lyrical, prophetic, and dramatic sources, old prayers and stories and laws, a new language has come into being that serves all the needs of everyday life. In vain the Irish have been trying to revive their ancient Celtic language. The Indians are still bogged down in their attempt to introduce a national language instead of the foreign English. But the Jewish people in Israel speaks and creates in its own ancient language. Even Herzl, the great visionary who outlined the most realistic plans for the transfer of millions by boat and by train and their deployment in agriculture and industry in a big *Eretz Israel,* irrigated by waterworks from the heights of Mount Hermon along the entire Jordan, even he questioned whether one would ever be able to ask for a railway ticket in Hebrew.

And then there is the socio-economic Zionist revolution. A nation which under diaspora conditions had neither a proper farming nor a proper working class had to develop a modern economy under difficult soil and climatic conditions and despite the obstacles posed by its own diaspora-taught, centuries-old habits.

And last but not least, what may be the most surprising aspect of the Zionist Revolution—astonishing to many of us and startling to the rest of the world—the Jews' achievements in the military field. But more about that later.

These are the various aspects of the Zionist revolution, but its essential core consists of the mass transfer of the Jewish people to its homeland. Try to imagine that in the country you are living in the population had grown three and a half times its original size within a space of twenty years. And try to imagine further that this took place while your country was in a state of war with its neighbours, and that it nevertheless maintained its democratic way of life. Can you conceive of the greatness of this feat? Anywhere else, would such an undertaking not result in turmoil and civil war?

We are not saying this in order to pat ourselves on the back. We are saying it with a view to the present and the future. Now that the Jews in the U.S.S.R. are fighting for their liberation there are some among us who ask with typical Jewish jocosity, (one part irony and two parts anxiety), what will happen if, God forbid, the Russians open their gates all at once and let all these millions of Jews out. How shall we take them in? What will happen here? That certainly need not be our main worry. The revolutionary Zionist is worried lest the opposite might happen. For him the real disaster is that the U.S.S.R. might open only a narrow gate to let no more than a few thousand go, in order to silence the outcry of the rest and take the wind out of the sails of the new Russian Jewish Revolution. This should be the primary concern of the Zionist movement and of the State of Israel, and not the pusillanimous fear lest all the millions may be released all at once. We were but 700,000 in 1948 when the State of Israel was established—700,000 who lacked the experience of independent statehood, with an underdeveloped economy, poor in natural resources except the natural or perhaps supernatural resources of the Jewish people as such and their willingness to rally to the task. Yet these 700,000 managed to take in close to two million, most of them without skill, occupation or education. How can we then doubt our capacity to take in at least a million Russian Jews most of whom are well equipped to function in a modern technological world? This is the new phase in the great Jewish Revolution which, generating its own momentum, will again work unforeseen wonders.

Herzl once replied to one of the skeptics who doubted his vision: An orange needs a table in order not to fall to the ground; Zionism is like the globe—it is kept up by its own motion. The existential need for a Jewish revolution is the only motive force required.

Zionism with its most precious instrument, the State of Israel, consequently is a revolutionary movement par excellence. It is such and must be such because the plight of the Jewish people brooks no delay. If we had heeded this imperative in the past and adopted the necessary revolutionary course we would by now have had at least 10 million in this country, and our achievements would have been many times as great.

There is another reason why the revolutionary character of Zionism needs special emphasis at this juncture. We have already spoken about the valuable resources of the Jewish nation that have gone to waste, down the drain of various socialist or alien national revolutions. We have also noted that one of the reasons for this was the idealistic and revolutionary character of these movements. There can be no doubt that the average Jew has a more highly developed sense of justice than the average gentile, and that our long and extensive history has given us a wider view and trained our youth for acts of greater daring.

One need not be a Jewish chauvinist. All that is needed is to get rid of the pervading feeling of self-hate, and be as objective as any scientist approaching his subject. If we do so we are forced to conclude that the Jewish people constitute a great nation, far greater than our mere numbers would seem to indicate (though 14 million are nothing to scoff at). This inherited greatness provokes an urge for great things. It cannot be satisfied with trivial deeds, especially since we are also endowed with a kind of holy impatience and restlessness that does not allow us to remain passive onlookers who let the world go its own way, at most giving good advice.

One of the failures of Zionism has been that it did not and still does not make sufficient use of the tremendous potential of our people, especially our youth.

Zionist chronicles tell the story of the emissary from *Eretz Israel* who came to a town in Russia—before the Revolution—and delivered a fiery harangue to the local Jewish youngsters that took all of two hours. And at the end of it, he asked them to donate 20 kopeks each (the equivalent of 20 cents) to a Zionist fund. "That's all?" piped up one of the youngsters. "Is that what you had to get us all excited about? I thought you were at least going to ask us to march along in formation and conquer *Eretz Israel* . . ."

There is much truth in this anecdote.

The greatest Hebrew contemporary poet, Uri Zvi Greenberg, expressed the same idea in his exhortation to the nation, written in 1933.

O NATION, HOW GREAT YOU ARE!
Even in captivity mounting to millions!
Your sons, broad of shoulder and strong in spirit,
Arms of iron, thighs of steel;
Sons to work the soil and make homes,
Sons to build houses and factories,
Bridges and tunnels, harbours and highways;
Sons marching to battle against the foe,
Striking the fear of their ancient race into his heart;
Sons to run trains, steer ships, pilot planes,
To sing Hebrew chanteys
In all the seaports of the world,
Wherever they put in with their cargoes;
Shades of sunset in their faces,
And the might of the sea in their eyes.

O Nation, your abundant daughters, lovely and sound,
Daughters to work in village and town;
Blessed, themselves, to branch forth like trees,
Giving birth to a new generation
Healthy and fair and tanned by the sun.
And from them—prophets and scholars,
Men of action and daring,
Rulers to take command.

What shall they do here today,
Your sons and daughters,
In the fullness of their vigour,
With the storm of their dammed-up fury,
The force of revolt within them?
What shall they do
With the pulse of battle pounding in their blood?

Bid them conquer the land,
Scale the peaks with standards flying;
Command them to go through fire,
Storm the walls of Titus, raze Bastilles;
As rebels they will go forth,
And you shall hear them, singing their song
Of freedom and conquest and redemption,
Full redemption!
Bid them span the deepest chasms,
And they will turn their bodies into bridges!
Bid them tear down a bridge,
And they will break their bodies with it!

Therefore, O Nation,
Are your sons and daughters walking the earth in anger;
Hundreds, thousands, with rage in their blood,
Bitter of soul, grinding their teeth,
Blaspheming the Kingdom and House of David and blessing the
    House of Stalin,
Trapped like tigers—so many silently expiring
In prisons, in the bloom of their youth,
Dragged off at sunrise to eternal sleep
In an alien land.

Can they be charged with betrayal?
No, it is not they who are guilty!
They are in need of men who are leaders,
Who like themselves are rebels in spirit
With rage in their blood.
They are in need of prophets
To march before them like pillars of fire,
In this—their own generation.

Translation: S.H.G. From "ODE TO THE NATION"
by Uri Zvi Greenberg, 1933.

This does not mean to say that donations and agricultural settlements were not an essential part of the programme. Nor do we want to imply that there were no difficulties in leaving the diaspora or in entering the country. But for various reasons the Zionist leadership gave in to these difficulties much too soon, settling into a comfortable routine of meeting immediate everyday needs. It preferred the easy course that did not call for any major conflict with the hostile British Mandatory government. Above all, it miscalculated the time factor.

Because of this easy-going manner in which the Zionist movement ambled along, it lost most of its potential. Other revolutions, that showed much greater impetus and elan, provided a better outlet for the bottled up energies of a dissatisfied young Jewish generation.

Zionism thus chose to stress its evolutionary, philanthropic or even experimental aspect. Sometimes it also assumed an idealistic-sentimentalist character. In doing so it failed to bring about a true Jewish revolution in the form of a mass transfer of an entire nation to a deserted country that should have been revived not only through the establishment of idyllic socialist kibbutzim, but could from the outset have become a major economic and cultural enterprise where the Jewish people might unfold its ramified talents to the full. This could have presented a major challenge, loftier and more difficult than the challenge presented by any of the revolutions then under way in Europe. Hundreds of youngsters actually experienced this let-down on coming to *Eretz Israel* and discovering the slow, pastoral fashion in which the Zionist ideal was being accomplished. They had come in the expectation of great things to be, and the mincing steps with which evolutionary Zionism moved, failed to satisfy their hunger for change and achievement.

At one time Zionist leaders went so far as to speak out against the idea of a Jewish state, concentrating all their efforts on bargaining with the British about another thousand or two thousand entry permits—certificates, as they were called —to *Eretz Israel,* the land of the Jews. At the same time there were thousands and tens of thousands of young Jews who did not want to spend years waiting for a certificate. The ground was burning under their feet and their hearts burning inside them. Zionism having become counter-revolutionary, they joined some other movement that still retained its revolutionary character.

It is hardly surprising that the change—in the diaspora as well as in *Eretz Israel*—came about only with the beginning of the underground struggle against the British Mandatory regime. The second turning point was the establishment of the State of Israel. Recently the movement once again shifted into a different gear, with the Six Day War. Evidently the impact of each of these revolutionary developments on the Jewish youngsters in the diaspora was much greater than the effect of solemn addresses or fund-raising campaigns, conducted in a spirit of philanthropy or idyllic sentimentality.

All this is not a matter of the past.

It is a matter of the present and the future. External threats and developments in the Jewish world again make it necessary to take a revolutionary course. The volcano is again beginning to rumble. Once more we are faced with the risk that we might be too late. And there are still, as always, Jewish youngsters in the world who want to do the great things they know they are capable of. The Jewish youngsters of the U.S.S.R. have already taken up the good fight.

Some of the Jewish youngsters of the West are fighting, too, but not their own battles. They are again immolating themselves for the sake of others, giving their best for the liberation of others. And however just and important these liberation movements may be—the liberation movement of the Jewish people, unequalled in beauty and justice, is more important.

The convolutions of history are strange. Israel's army is

again facing the Egyptian army in the very same place where the first exodus took place under the leadership of Moses. But in the meantime the front has spread out to many other places as well. The role of Egypt the enslaver has in our times been filled by Nazi Germany and by Stalinist and Neo-Stalinist Russia, the one throwing our children into the fire, the other not letting our people go. The first scene of the drama—Joseph's days of greatness in Egypt—is being re-enacted elsewhere, in America. And Russia, trying to prevent the exodus, is lending a hand to the Egyptian pseudo-pharaohs of today.

Thus on the contemporary stage all three acts of our ancient drama are being produced simultaneously: Prosperity in a foreign land; Enslavement; Exodus and the liberation of our country. We are re-living the days of Joseph, Moses, Joshua and David, all at once. Thanks to this concurrence of events our generation has the potential of being the greatest of all. It can experience an unprecedented physical and spiritual growth not unlike that which took place after the Egyptian exodus. For Jewish statehood can and will accomplish the threefold task: saving our people from the imminent threat of destruction, liberating its homeland, and bringing about a national renaissance. All three are closely interrelated. A great country for a great nation is the physical and economic basis for that nation's spiritual renaissance.

6

RIGHT NECESSARY AND POSSIBLE

TRUTH is clear and straightforward. Falsehood has a thousand devious faces; outwardly often bright, inside it is hollow and brittle like glass. Truth is beautiful. Falsehood tries to be. Clarity and simplicity do not detract from the wholeness and beauty of truth. Nor does versatility make up for the essential poverty and ugliness of falsity.

Assimilation is ugly. It is an affectation and therefore false. Above all, it is an act of desertion.

Nor is it wise, for it implies defection from a great past, present and future—the past and present of the Jewish people and the wonderful future that lies before it.

Zionism is beautiful. No liberation movement has ever been more so. The spectacle of a nation whose long and colourful history ranges from the peaks of Sinai, the Kremlin, the Davidic kingdom—to the abyss of Auschwitz; a nation that has brought forth such men as Moses, Jesus, Marx, the Baal Shem Tov the founder of Hassidism, and Trotsky the father of the Red Army,—now returning to its ancestral homeland, and to its ancient language; such a nation remains unmatched and unequaled. Can there be anything more beautiful than the conversion of a people that was only recently driven like sheep to the slaughter, setting up its own victorious army; than the leap from the Talmud school to the Weizmann Institute of Science known for its nuclear and biological research; or from the fiddler on the ramshackle roof of the diaspora that threatens to cave in or burn down at any moment while he is plucking his strings to the Israel Philharmonic Orchestra; from the stock exchange to the kibbutz; from "luftgeschaeften" to a real aircraft industry and airforce! Can there be anything lovelier than the sight of the exiles from seventy-seven lands of dispersion fusing into one single whole in one single state!

It is all the more beautiful because this act of return is no utopian attempt to produce something out of nothing. It is based on the firm ground of reality: The spirit and matter of the Jewish people, which has never ceased to exist throughout the diaspora, and sustained the belief in its potential and ultimate revival, is being converted into a new, modern being.

Numberless dogmas and doctrines have been upset. Countless false gods and utopias have failed. Zionism has outlived them all and remained triumphant; not the paltry, philanthropic variety aspiring to a national, spiritual-cultural centre, not the Zionism of one-more-acre and one-more-tree, not that which strove to build a haven for poor Jewish refugees, but precisely the revolutionary, messianic brand of political-territorial Zionism.

All this was not accomplished in any miraculous, mystical fashion. The very existence of the Jewish nation may be a miracle in the sense that it runs counter to the natural processes of history. Its salvation, however, which many had been envisaging as a miraculous event, is proceeding in the most natural and realistic fashion through the reshaping of the land and the people and the establishment of a new reality in a mighty gust of greatness.

But we have already spoken about Satan who in his mean and grudgeful way is trying to foil this godly undertaking. The guises he puts on to achieve his ends are many. He may appear in the guise of piety and humanitarianism, of kindness and of justice—all in order to stem the course of ultimate salvation. Sometimes—and then he is most dangerous—he wears the mask of a Zionist and acts as a fifth columnist within the Zionist movement and the State of Israel, twisting the nation's heart and mind, and confusing its leaders and youth. By thus entangling the healthy forest of the nation in a sickly undergrowth he gives renewed hope to our enemies: perhaps they may yet frustrate our salvation.

From time to time it is therefore necessary to take the axe to this jungle undergrowth, and once again let the clear, simple truth be heard so that Satan's work may be undone.

This we shall do here for three types of such undergrowth, such misguided concepts and ideas which have recurred at each and every decisive stage in the progress of the Zionist movement.

On the face of it the circumstances may have been different, but the psychological error has always been the same; the gnawing doubt, despair and negation were the same. Now they have again reappeared with regard to the right of the Jewish people to the whole of *Eretz Israel,* and its ability to hold on to it.

Those who renege on the revolutionary, redemptionary character of Zionism may be divided into three groups:

The group that says it is wrong.
The group that says it is unnecessary.
The group that says it is impossible.

During the Early Stages of Zionism

When the idea of the Return to Zion was first conceived, cries of moral outrage were heard from many sides. Even orthodox Jews who had never sought emancipation and assimilation put in their veto. They did not veto the underlying idea, which was essentially the same messianic idea they espoused, but the way in which it was to be accomplished. Salvation cannot be man-made, they said. One must wait for a miracle from heaven, for the Messiah, the son of David.

Orthodox Jewry insisted Zionism was wrong because it was afraid that like the Shabtai Zvi movement it might lead to mass conversion. Of this brand only a small handful is left now, the Naturei Karta group in Jerusalem and the Sattmer Hassids in Williamsburg. In their favour it may be said that at least their intentions were good. They never ceased to believe in the Jewish people and its salvation; their opposition stemmed from this very concern, because they deplored Zionism's secular methods.

Worse was the opposition of liberal Judaism. Apart from a small minority, most of the members of this group also vetoed the Zionist conception. It was wrong because all that talk about Jewish nationalism ran counter to the essential dogma of the Jewish emancipation movement—national assimilation. We are Germans in Germany, Frenchmen in France, Americans (??) in America, they said. The only difference is that we are members of the Mosaic faith—of a religion, not a national group. Of that religion, too, fairly little was left; no more than a rather transparent veneer with the ardent desire for assimilation showing through. At any rate, that is how it was then.

The liberals were also outraged because they felt Zionism would help the anti-Semites, who claimed the Jews were not loyal to the nations they were living amongst because their hearts and minds were turned to Zion. The anti-Semites kept saying that Jewish solidarity went beyond territorial borders, that the Jews constituted a single alien entity transcending nationalities and states. The Jews could therefore never be true patriots, and so the gentile nations had no need of them. They were very much *de trop* and should be removed! And here come the Zionists and confirm all these things and are actually willing to help the anti-Semites in achieving their ends!

That most of the Left—the Communists more than the Socialists, of course—were against Zionism, is obvious. They too, screamed that it was wrong, wrong because it ran counter to the Marxist doctrine that nationalism is a product of the class war and that once class differences are abolished national distinctions are bound to disappear. They also objected because the Jewish revolutionary potential might be diverted to a "narrow-minded" national course. Because Zionism harks back to age-old roots it was naturally branded as a reactionary movement. It is wrong, they said, because it strengthens the Right and leans on rightist, reactionary and imperialist movements.

When Zionism, despite all these vetoes developed into a mass movement that set about accomplishing its ideals, when it won international recognition (whether for humanitarian reasons or as a means of getting rid of the "surplus" Jews); when nationality became a dominant element in Europe, and when the Left was unable to prevent national developments even in its own ranks; when the Left could at most aspire to internationalism but not to a cosmopolitanism that transcends nationality; then came the second reservation:

Granted that Zionism is not wrong, that the Jews too have a *right* to be a nation, that they are entitled to strive for political independence—*what* on earth do they *need* it for?

Zionism contended that not only was there a need for it, but that it was essential in order to safeguard the physical and spiritual existence of the nation. The threats were such as to make it imperative.

Liberal and leftist elements were not concerned about the spiritual existence of the Jewish people, nor are they to this day. Regarding its physical existence, they argued that in these modern times annihilation was inconceivable. If modern enlightenment afforded no general protection, at least it could not happen "here," not in Germany with its high standard of education and culture, or in the (still) pluralistic United States of America. Any physical threats there might have been in pogrom-ridden Eastern Europe were removed by the Revolution, so that the Jews there no longer needed saving. The world was making progress, becoming more liberal, more egalitarian, and certainly more civilised; so no minority need live in fear of its life. Thus they kept on protesting until Hitler and Stalin came to prove the contrary. Liberalism failed, Socialism failed—but before they were defeated millions of Jews were defeated too, in a most finite way. Nor did Communism prove immune to anti-Semitism.

Zionism, far from being unnecessary, proved to be a primary necessity, a categorical imperative.

But granting even that, was it feasible? Could millions of Jews from so many countries be simply transferred to one country, especially if that country was not totally uninhabited either? Would the various powers or the local inhabitants agree to such a move? Could the Jews be welded into a single entity with one language? Could a nation of merchants and writers be turned into a nation of farmers and workers? Could this nation, which has not managed its own political affairs for close to two thousand years, organize a modern state of its own? And above all, could Jews be turned into soldiers who would be able to defend themselves on their own? Are the Jews not naturally fearful and cringing, repelled by the very idea of bloodshed and bearing arms?

The Jews proved to be greater skeptics than the gentiles. Profound self-contempt and self-belittlement were their worst enemies. They had begun to believe in the slanders the gentiles had spread about them; in their political and military ineptitude, their abhorrence of physical labour.

"It may be permissible and essential; it may even be beautiful; but are not all fairy tales beautiful? So what?" they asked.

Came Herzl and said: If you want it so, it will be no fairy tale. It will be real.

What turned out to be a fairy tale were the seemingly realistic Communist and Socialist visions of equality, justice and peace among nations. What was initially regarded as a daring flight of fancy, a piece of Jewish messianic mysticism —that the Jews should want and be able to return to their country—turned out to be the only realistic part of the drama.

It turned out to be realistic because it was not only a right but a duty, not only a necessity but an imperative need. Above all, it was possible. The State of Israel is a living fact.

On the Way to Statehood

When the imperative need for Zionism and its feasibility had been proven, Satan again tried one of his tricks, again assuming Zionist garb.

Fundamentally, as stated, Zionism is the ancient messianic ideal supplemented by modern techniques. Its goal is and was the salvation of the entire Jewish people and the liberation of the Jewish homeland. This obviously meant that *Eretz Israel* should become a free and independent Jewish state. At various stages, Zionism found it necessary, for tactical and diplomatic reasons, not to state its goal in this overt fashion. Thus the Balfour Declaration (after the Zionist leaders had lobbied for it in these terms) spoke of a national "home" for the Jewish people. These subterfuges, however, soon turned out to be worse than useless. The Arabs began to obstruct the course of Zionism the moment the Balfour Declaration was issued, and the British made use of the ambiguities in its text to curtail immigration and settlement. There was an imminent danger that we would really end up with a kind of "national home," housing an insignificant Jewish minority deprived of sovereignty, and that the full exodus from the diaspora could thus never take place, especially as many Zionists had come to believe in the reduced version of the ideal that they had initially expounded solely for reasons of expediency. It was then that

Jabotinsky founded the national Zionist organisation, with its youth movement, Betar, which in turn gave rise to two underground movements—the IZL or the National Military Organization (Irgun), and the FFI, the Fighters for the Freedom of Israel.

Jabotinsky and his followers thus reaffirmed the triple platform of classical Zionism:

1. Zionism means a Jewish state within the historical boundaries of Eretz Israel, on both sides of the Jordan.
2. Zionism means the evacuation of the threatened diasporas.
3. Zionism implies a revival of the Jewish fighting spirit and may involve actual warfare for the liberation of the country.

And again these three claims were countered with the same three No's: they are wrong, unnecessary and impossible.

Wrong—because we must not say outright that we intend to set up a Jewish State. This will only increase Arab hostility to the step-by-step settlement of the country and the drop-by-drop immigration of Jews.

Wrong—because a declaration of that kind will scare off Jewish donors, especially in America, who object to political Zionism and are only willing to support a philanthropic, spiritual version of the idea, for fear of getting involved in problems of dual loyalty.

And even if it is not wrong, what is it good for? The constructive enterprise of building up the country can proceed just as well under the auspices of the British mandate, without political sovereignty; that is something we might perhaps achieve by slow easy steps at the end of this process. For the time being all we need is to grow and slowly consolidate.

Granted also that it is both permissible and necessary—

is it possible? The Arabs are against it, the British are against it. We are a minority in this country. England is a huge empire, and the Arabs are so many!

A letter written by Haim Arlozoroff a socialist Zionist leader, who was murdered in 1933, apparently by Arabs, with or without the connivance of the British, came to light in 1948. Arlozoroff had written that in order to save the Zionist undertaking it was necessary to take over the government, to set up a Jewish state on the whole western side of the Jordan and to place it under Jewish military command while opening the gates of the country to free immigration until we become a majority. The letter was written when there were only 180,000 Jews in the country. It was addressed to Haim Weizmann, the President of the Zionist Organisation. Although violent methods might conflict with some of our principles—added Arlozoroff—if the choice lies between them and the implementation of Zionism, "I had rather see us give up these principles, because the people's salvation depends on it."

Arlozoroff's proposal remained a complete secret between him and Weizmann (unless, of course, the British got to know about it) and suddenly he was killed—by whom?

Arlozoroff was a moderate, realistic Zionist. Had his proposal been carried out at the time, the Jews of Europe could have been evacuated before the Second World War.

This was the irreparable error of those who rejected the programme of political Zionism with what had by then become the habitual refrain: "Wrong, Unnecessary, Impossible."

It was not only right: It was a sacred duty.
It was not only necessary: It was an imperative.
And—it was certainly possible.

For again there was no lack of conscientious objectors. A group of college professors, under the leadership of Martin Buber, denounced any military measures which were, according to their peculiar interpretation, contrary to the spirit of Judaism. They were also opposed on principle to any active retaliation to Arab rioting. Revenge, they claimed, was foreign to the spirit of Judaism. They preferred the Jews to be the victims who would then appeal to the conscience of the world or, like in the diaspora, apply to the gentile, British police for protection.

Then there were those who again said it was not necessary because the mandatory regime was responsible for civil security and matters should be left in its hands.

Many of those who conceded that action might be necessary claimed that it was impossible. How could we stand up to such superior forces? Would we not thereby jeopardise the entire Jewish community already living in this country (Palestine)?

In the thirties, moreover, it was only too easy to denounce as a fascist anyone who wanted a Jewish state and a Jewish army. It was accepted as a matter of course that a nation should have a state and an army and should fight for its freedom; that is, every other nation but the Jews.

When the Second World War broke out and it became evident that Great Britain had betrayed the trust of the League of Nations and reneged on its pledge under the Balfour Declaration, closing the gates of the country to the refugees from Hitler's horrors, sinking their ships and declaring a moratorium on the Jewish homeland by condemning the Jews to being a permanent minority, the Zionist establishment was finally aroused from its slumber. Then it too began to talk about the need for a Jewish State (Ben Gurion's declaration at the Biltmore Conference in 1941) and for taking up arms, either in the ranks of the armies already fighting the Nazis or in order to ward off a possible German attack against the country. It was for this second purpose that the Palmach was formed, with the aid of the British. The Zionist establishment woke up too late, however, to be able to rescue the Jews of Europe.

In the meantime the FFI and the IZL had come into

being, a fighting underground determined to liberate the country from the British occupiers, and establish an independent Jewish state after the liberation had been accomplished.

Needless to say, the same three arguments cropped up again: It is *wrong*, because the British are the lawful rulers by international resolution. It is *wrong* because if the British leave we shall be left alone among a sea of Arabs. It is *unnecessary* because once Hitler is vanquished the world will be free, justice will triumph and we too shall get our just deserts. It is *unnecessary* because England will have a Labour government and the Labour party has pledged the reopening of the country to immigration.

And thirdly, it is *impossible*. How can we, who are so few, drive out the British, an imperial power, which has 100,000 paratroopers stationed in this country alone!

The War came to an end. Great Britain continued its anti-Zionist policy, firmly intent on handing the country over to the Arabs. Ernest Bevin's Labour government was worse than its Conservative predecessors. The refugees from the extermination camps, who had managed to make the exodus were returned to DP—"displaced persons"—camps in Germany, or exiled to Maritius. Many were imprisoned and some were shot and killed or drowned.

Clearly there was no option but to fight for independence. But was it possible?

The gentiles had proved that fight we *must*. IZL and the FFI proved that we *can*.

From its inception Zionism had been a national liberation movement, and the adoption of military means for the attainment of that end had been suggested from the start. When the British mooted a Jewish settlement in Cyprus, as far back as 1901, Herzl considered it as a possible base for the invasion of *Eretz Israel* should the Turkish Sultan, who was then ruling the country, be unwilling to allow Jewish mass settlement. In World War I, Joseph Trumpeldor, the socialist-Zionist revolutionary who was the founder of the *Hechalutz* (The Pioneer) Movement, intended to raise a Jewish army of 100,000 in the crumbling Czarist Empire and invade *Eretz Israel* via the Caucasus and Syria in order to establish a *fait accompli*. He was too late, because the October Revolution intervened, disrupting communications and sowing confusion among the people, including the Jews. The Betar movement was set up in order to provide the core of the military forces that would be needed when the day of the revolt came. On the eve of the Second World War, Abraham Stern ("Yair"), the founder of the FFI, began to organize an army of 40,000 in Poland, on behalf of the IZL, for an armed invasion.

He also came too late. The outbreak of the War foiled his scheme through which six millions might have been saved. It was not too late for the Jewish community of *Eretz Israel,* numbering about 650,000, nor for the ten million Jews in the rest of the world, especially in certain countries, where they were already threatened with extinction.

Thus, however long it tarried, the Jewish Liberation Movement finally adopted the essential course of a War of Liberation—the only right and possible course to attain its goal of complete salvation for the Jewish people.

It was a course that proved its usefulness against the British and against the Arabs, and will again be the only effective course on the new front that has recently opened —against the oppression of the Jews in the Soviet Union.

7

THE ZIONIST FRONT IN SOVIET RUSSIA

1. The Causes of Russian Anti-Zionism

"I felt that Russia's expansion was arousing alarm and made immediate use of this fact. I explained that Russia was behind Turkey's opposition and that clearly Russia was trying to expand to Asia Minor until she will suddenly be on the shores of the Mediterranean, and it is only then that Zionism will be lost. Only when Eretz Israel falls into Russian hands will we forfeit our hopes to regain it."

(Herzl, Diaries, January 3, 1901)

H ERZL'S farsightedness and the justification of his anxiety stand fully revealed in the perspective of seventy years. Luckily the Russian bear failed to sink his claws into this area before the Jewish people had managed to lay the firm foundations for its renewed statehood there. Had the Russians got here first, they would no doubt have frustrated our efforts.

Needless to say, the Communist Russian regime is much more dangerous than its Czarist predecessor. The Czarist cavalry, the notorious Black Hundred of the imperial police and the savage, drunken moujiks of those times were as nothing compared to Stalin's hammer and sickle or Khrushchev's boot or Kosygin and Brezhniev's Neo-Stalinism—for whom the trampling and destruction of a nation is a minor interlude.

Though Zionism lost the race against the Nazis, it is still not too late to forestall the Soviet menace.

Geopolitically Russia's southern expansionism now is not much different from what it was in Czarist times. Then the places holy to the Russian Orthodox Church served as an excuse. The present ploy is her deep concern for the oppressed Arab refugees under the cudgel of Jewish-Zionist imperialism. The outward guise matters little. At most it serves to dress up the figures appearing in that ridiculous, hypocritical charade referred to as the U.N.

Historically, and particularly from the Jewish point of view, the Soviet peril, however, is much greater than were the dangers of Czarist Russian imperialism.

There are four reasons for the Soviets' inveterate hostility to Zionism and the State of Israel:

The first reason is of a fundamental, dogmatic nature. Though the Soviet Union is an empire with distinct imperialistic aspirations, it is nevertheless much more Communist than Czarist Russia ever was Greek Orthodox. Communism has always been essentially anti-Zionist. Marx and Lenin, its original theoreticians, denied the existence of a Jewish nation. With Marx, the baptised Jew, this repudiation was mixed with a goodly measure of personal animosity. Not so with Lenin, whose theoretical reasons were, however, not unmixed with practical considerations of expediency. He needed the brains and ability, the dedication and zeal of Jewish intellectuals and youth for the dissemination of the Communist creed in Europe. Owing to external circumstances and their own inner leanings these were the circles that were ripe for Marxism and the Communist Revolution. Zionism was a rival force competing for these Jewish elements. Hence Lenin's insistence on the negation of the Jewish national collective.

Unfortunately, he found ready helpers in the Communist Jews; whether from true conviction or out of servility and self-hate these auto-vivisectionists were already responsible for the persecution of the *Hehalutz* Zionist pioneering Movement and of Zionism even in the early days of the Russian Revolution.

On the theoretical side a further consideration is the Communist claim to provide the solution to all problems of segregation and discrimination. Communism wants to have a monopoly on the salvation of the oppressed. If the Russian Jews were to seek their salvation elsewhere, it would mean that the Soviet Union was not the land of salvation it pretends to be.

In this respect there is some resemblance between Communism and the Christian Church. The Jewish Return to Zion contradicts the Christian article of faith that Jesus was the Messiah the Prophets had been talking about—Christ being the Greek word for Messiah.

Although Communism has shown considerable flexibility with regard to many of its doctrines, the dogma repudiating Zionism as a Jewish national liberation movement undoubtedly still stands.

The second reason is connected with foreign policy—the position the U.S.S.R. has adopted as the backer and supporter of the Arab states, ostensibly as the champion of "liberation movements to throw off the yoke of imperialism." What the holy places were to the Czars of yesterday, these so-called liberation movements have become to the Red imperialism of today. Geography persists, despite internal political changes. Geopolitical, economic and military interests supervene, seeking their outlet, and looking for an excuse to do so. That the Arab states are opposed to Zionism and the State of Israel, can be nicely wrapped up in phrases about the liberation of nations from imperialist suppression, especially since it fits in so well with the anti-Zionist principle. Since, moreover, the U.S.A. happens to be for Zionism and Israel, the self-evident conclusion is that the U.S.S.R. must be against.

The argument that the U.S.S.R. supported the establishment of the State of Israel in 1947 hardly holds water. Had it not been for the underground struggle to oust the British from *Eretz Israel*—the beginning of their ouster from the entire Middle East—the U.S.S.R. would never have given its support. The Soviets jumped on this bandwagon at the time in order to consummate the British evacuation of the Middle East and gain a foothold there themselves, lest the U.S.A. might fill the vacuum.

This was no reversal of policy and of doctrine. The U.S.S.R. persisted in its hostility to Zionism. In line with dialectical practice it recognized the existing fact of the Jewish State, which seemed a convenient lever for further intervention on its part.

The FFI, the Fighters for the Freedom of Israel, rightly insisted on the neutralisation of the Middle East, with total non-intervention in the conflict with the Arab states, should it continue. There no longer can be any doubt that without Soviet intervention, not only would the State of Israel by now have been greater and stronger, but the Arab states would have made their peace with it. Had it not been for Soviet support, they would long since have become reconciled to it, and the entire map would have been different, and hardly to our disadvantage. The neutralisation and non-intervention scheme, however, was not carried out. We are therefore forced to seek whatever allies we can and whichever are best for us. Even so we have become the hardest nut for the Soviets to crack in their present push into the Middle East.

The third reason for Soviet anti-Zionism is associated with internal politics. The renaissance of the Soviet Jews after the establishment of the State of Israel and the appearance of our ambassadors, the new impetus given by the Six Day War, Israeli singers and sports teams, bore all the hallmarks of a messianic revival only rarely equalled in the history of the diaspora.

The demand for a mass exodus proved a major embarrassment to the Soviet regime. It can rightly claim that in not letting them go it practices no discrimination against the Jews, other Soviet citizens being equally barred from leaving the country *en masse*. Any relaxation of this rule with respect to the Jews, it is feared, might start a chain reaction among others. Against this it can be validly argued that the Jews are not like the other minorities in the U.S.S.R., which after all have their national territorial existence assured to them in their own homeland while the Jews are deprived in that respect, as they regard *Eretz Israel* as their homeland. It is not unlikely that ultimately this argument will be advanced, if not by us then by the Soviets themselves; but in the meantime their fear of potential mass emigration is growing. An added consideration is that a Jewish mass exodus would be a tacit admission of the error of Lenin's thesis regarding the Jewish people and Zionism.

Also, as long as the Russians maintain their strongly pro-Arab line, preventing the mass emigration of Jews is part of the support they are giving to the Arab States. (For some reason they do not assume that the Jews, once allowed to settle in Israel, would turn into Communist agents intent on propagating the Communist gospel in the Middle East!)

The dogmatic ideological tenets as well as the considerations of foreign and domestic policy are all three imbedded in a fourth, irrational motive—the deep-seated Russian hatred of the Jews. Anti-Semitism cannot be wiped out either by law or by theory. Its historical, sociological and psychological roots go far too deep. From the same roots that recently once again brought forth the term "Judash" derive many other anti-Jewish Soviet manifestations, from the "doctors' plot" in Stalin's time down to the horror propaganda now being disseminated in books and caricatures which might have come straight off Goebbel's printing-blocks. This is an irrational motive far removed from Marxist and Communist rationalism. That the Kremlin's leaders knew how to play on it seems highly indicative of their personal involvement. They were well aware that anti-Semitic incitement is just as effective in Communist Russia as it was in Czarist, feudal or capitalist Russia, and Jew-baiting is no less popular a sport.

Among the psychological causes we must also include the Soviets' dismay at the revolutionary attitude taken by the Jews, and their indignation at the Jews having dared to tear off the mask of a regime that prides itself on being a human paradise yet deprives its subjects of the most elementary right—the right to leave. Underlying all these factors is the growing frustration since the Six Day War. Not only were Russia's allies beaten despite their Soviet arms, but more recently Soviet planes flown by Russian pilots were downed.

For all these reasons Russia is engaged in an active war against the Jewish people of the U.S.S.R. and against their state—Israel.

2. The Jewish Revolution in the U.S.S.R.

It is under these conditions that the Jews of Russia are conducting a tremendous revolution. Under a Communist dictatorship they openly dare to identify with the State of Israel and with the Zionist cause. Their defiance and daring may well be compared to the martyrdom of previous generations of Jews in the name of their faith and their God.

The most startling aspect of this revolution is that it is not made by the older Jews, born and reared in traditional Jewish communities and homes, or the Jews living in the Western provinces annexed by Russia only after the Second World War, who still grew up in a Jewish-Zionist atmosphere. It is made by the younger generation that has been bred by the Communist regime. Moreover, in spite of restrictions imposed by the authorities, and a substratum of latent anti-Semitism, no gross discrimination has been practiced. Most of these Jewish fighters are well-educated people doing well in their chosen professions. Their motivation is purely ideological. Their revolt stems from sheer Jewish-Zionist patriotism, that needed no stimulation by emissaries from this country.

We are thus confronted with a new historical development. While hitherto Zionism stemmed from two sources— the positive source of eternal Jewish longing for salvation and the negative source of anti-Semitism—which joined to bring about the establishment of the State of Israel, now the State of Israel has become the main inspiration. In a Communist state, Israel triumphant has become the mainspring for admiration and longing and the desire to return to Zion. Not only do the Russian Jews make a point of listening to the Israeli broadcasts over Kol Zion Lagola, of learning Hebrew and Jewish songs, but they write Hebrew poems of their own which are more moving in their simplicity than any we have here.

They are elemental Zionists, without any of our complexes and apologetics. Concepts and emotions that have been turned to ridicule here have attained a new significance over there. It is they who are teaching us once again the true nature of Zionism, re-inspiring our own youth that has grown contemptuous and cynical.

For years an inexcusable policy of hushing up what was going on among the Russian Jews was followed in Israel. Ostensibly this conspiracy of silence was for their own benefit, to enable a small trickle of them to get out, a conspiracy which the Russians cunningly exploited to ensure that silence. In fact world Jewry was sacrificed to the interests of the State of Israel, but not its real interests. This was in line with a general tendency to regard the State of Israel as the end-all and be-all of Zionism, the end of the road, which implied the abandonment of the Zionist ideal.

But the Communists and the Jews of the U.S.S.R. showed that this severance between Israelis and Jews could not be maintained. They showed that there were no separate fronts in this war, one Jewish and one Israeli. It is one single war fought on both fronts.

Just as the Arabs recalled us to the whole of *Eretz Israel*, the Soviet Communists prevented us from betraying the Jewish people and our own destiny.

3. The Youngsters of Zion

As stated, all those young Jewish engineers and doctors and students in Russia who have raised the flag of revolt are doing so of their own free will. They have the choice of remaining alienated from their people and living in relative prosperity and peace, without risking their life and liberty and social status.

Nevertheless they prefer to fight for their Jewishness and their right to return home, *"habaita,"* to *Eretz Israel*.

In this context it might be worthwhile mentioning one of the most famous anti-Semitic works—"The Protocols of the Elders of Zion." This book appeared in 1905, pretending to be the proceedings of a secret session at the First Zionist Congress held in Basle in 1897, at which the Jewish leaders mapped out a scheme for attaining world domination. Reprinted in innumerable editions and translations, it became a main source of anti-Semitic propaganda for many decades, in spite of irrefutable evidence furnished by the Swiss courts that it is nothing but a forgery. Nasser in Egypt, like Hitler, still used a refurbished Arab version to foment hostility against Israel.

The book was written by one Sergius Nilus (!) and first published in Czarist Russia.

Needless to say that the Elders of Zion never existed. The ideology evolved at the First Zionist Congress in Basle was diametrically opposed to the alleged resolutions of the Elders of Zion. Instead, the foundation was laid for the establishment of a Jewish State, a centrifugal movement designed to do away with the dispersion of the Jews and their role as beneficiaries and benefactors of the world. The very idea was no longer to furnish Marxes and Disraelis to the gentiles but to turn the entire forces of the Jewish people upon itself for the attainment of its independence and its return to Zion. The goal was self-government rather than ruling over others or being ruled by them.

There still remained Jews who repudiated this idea and continued to save the world from capitalism and imperialism and other real or imaginary evils, mounting barricades on behalf of others in the mistaken belief that they were doing so for their own sake as well. But Hitler and Stalin put an end to these illusions. And finally the State of Israel and its triumphs gave rise to a movement of the Youngsters of Zion.

Paradoxically enough, at the same time as the young Jews of the U.S.S.R., who have been brought up under a Leftist regime—and seen it in action—are up in arms against its ideas and want to go *home,* the Jews of the New Left in Paris and Berkeley are up in arms to perpetuate their exilic existence. In their defection from their own popular front, their rootless cosmopolitanism and their self-hate, it is they who personify the diaspora Jew.

Yet even the affluent, complacent Jews of the West and the younger generation stricken by the Joseph complex have not remained untouched by the spontaneous Jewish awakening of the Youngsters of Zion in Russia. The Jewish Defense League is the first sign of a similar movement in the West. Both unite into one single liberation front of the Jewish people, and bear the seed of a new mass exodus. This younger contingent, from Vladivostok to Los Angeles, provides a major reinforcement for the Jewish bastion already existing in *Eretz Israel.* Thanks to them we may rise to further pinnacles of achievement; for tremendous challenges still await us.

8

INTERMEZZO
RHAPSODY
CAESURA

1. Intermezzo – The Fighters for the Freedom of Israel (FFI)

IN a brief review of the fundamental problems of political Zionism there is no justification for going into isolated issues. Nevertheless I permit myself a brief digression. There was one chapter in the Jewish War of Liberation which was not only of objective significance, but was of personal importance to me, as an immediate participant: the FFI underground movement that fought the British during the 1940-1948 period. In singling out the FFI it is not intended to detract from the role played by any of the other organizations. Many of their operations were much too big for a small group like the FFI, which could but pay homage to those others who managed to carry them off. In fact, we shall not go into the operational side at all, but shall stress only one ideological-political innovation introduced by the small FFI group, because of its lasting relevance.

The FFI was one of the offshoots of Zeév Jabotinsky's political-national Zionist trend, the Betar youth movement and the IZL. It was founded by Abraham Stern who was murdered by the British in 1942. The smallest of the various underground movements, it was also the most radical and daring.*

---

*For further information on the FFI the English-speaking reader is referred to Gerald Frank's excellent book, *The Deed*, Simon and Schuster 1963.–Ed.

Its most distinctive feature, however, was the new political conception it evolved. So far, the political foundation on which the Zionist movement had relied in its fund-raising campaigns, and the execution of its programme had been the British Mandate and the Balfour Declaration. Great Britain had undertaken to help the Jewish people to set up its national home in this country. The Zionist establishment of that period did its very best to make use of the opportunities afforded by the British mandatory regime, driving a hard bargain for every immigration certificate and every acre of land to be purchased, for every new autonomous Jewish institution. It was in this way that most of the new settlements were established.

The activist opposition appreciated all these efforts, but did not think they went far enough. This, it contended, was only part of what had to be done. It was also more aware of the dangers threatening European Jewry and the need for rapid evacuation. Moreover, this nationalist opposition demanded active resistance to the Arab terror—and offered such resistance on its own. It believed that a Jewish military force and a more aggressive policy would convince the British that we were a lively factor on the scene, and that it would not pay them to give in to Arab extortion at our expense.

The revolutionary innovation of the FFI, its new political conception, was first publicised in the trials conducted against its members for their anti-British actions. They refused to participate in these trials on the grounds that the British courts had no legal standing in this country, which is the Land of Israel. The British are a foreign, imperialist occupying power, and the British Mandate granted by the League of Nations—the forerunner of the U.N.—cannot supersede the *a-priori* title of the Jewish nation to this land.

Eretz Israel is the land of the people of Israel whose title to it never lapsed. Any non-Jewish regime in this country is *ipso facto* foreign, whether it be favourably or unfavourably disposed to the Jews. It was not purely the restrictions imposed on immigration that the FFI objected to; they were up in arms against the very fact that the British should control the entry of Jews to this country.

"When our forefathers"—as the FFI defendants declared in court—"were living in this country with their kings and generals, their poets and prophets, the ancestors of the British were still living in the primeval forests of the savage British isles. Any Jew living in Brooklyn or in Moscow has more rights to this country than any foreign ruler who happens to be here. The use of British arms in *Eretz Israel* is unlawful and unjust. We, the fighters for the freedom of Israel, are the only ones entitled to bear arms, to fight for our rights. We want this country to be liberated for the Jewish people, not only because the Jews are being persecuted in the diaspora, and annihilated in Auschwitz. We would want it no less if they were living there in peace and plenty, for those are all foreign lands, countries of exile. This is the homeland of the Jewish people, this is where it first became a productive and creative nation. It was banished from here by force, and will therefore return by force. We are a Hebrew liberation movement."

This was a revolutionary new orientation. The struggle no longer revolved around the enforcement of resolutions and promises made by other nations. Instead, it was directed towards the implementation of the sovereign will and law of the Jewish people to be in possession of their own land and exercise its exclusive natural and historic right to this country.

I can already discern many readers wondering—is not that the same thing the Arabs are claiming, too? We shall go into this question more thoroughly further on, but in this context let me recount one telling episode from the time I spent in the central prison of Jerusalem for my underground activities in the FFI.

One day in June 1944 one of the senior commanders of the Nazi-controlled Arab underground, Dr. Husseini, was arrested and brought to the Central Gaol. A lawyer and a doctor, fluent in five languages, he had been sent to stir up trouble by his cousin, the grand mufti Hajj Amin El-Husseini who was at that time sitting in Berlin as the Nazi adviser on Middle Eastern and Jewish problems. Since I was wounded, Dr. Husseini would come into my cell every morning to bring me a cup of coffee and discuss politics. It was from him that I heard the most realistic analysis of the Israel-Arab conflict: We, the Arabs and the Jews, are having a legitimate dispute about this country, but what are the British doing here? They are certainly outsiders and must be expelled. Then there will be a war between the Jews and the Arabs. Whoever wins—the country is his!

I do not know where this Arab leader is today, but where we have got so far according to his prescription I do know. We have managed to oust the British—we, the Jewish and not the Arab underground. And we have defeated the Arabs, and if they continue the fight we shall beat them again.

We are not a foreign colonial power here, but the sons and inheritors of this land. We cannot be driven out. These are the existential facts. As for the merits of our claim, the moral ethical aspect that seems to bother many, especially in Western countries (some of them quite innocently and sincerely) we shall come back to it in one of the following chapters.

But the chief moral of the FFI intermezzo is that this movement did not pretend to be putting up a defence, to act in response to riots and provocations. Our problem in this country was not the defence of Jewish lives. Jews in the diaspora are also required to protect their life and honour. The authorities did not and still do not always adequately protect the Jewish community against malefactors and rioters, either because they are equally anti-Semitic as was the case in Russia or in Poland, or because they are powerless—as has been and still is the case in many Western democracies.

Here in *Eretz Israel*, however, it is not a question of putting up a defence against pogroms and riots. It is a question of liberating the country from any non-Jewish rule, from anyone who interferes with the return to Zion. It is a question of reconquering and liberating a homeland that has been taken from us by force but which we have never given up.

The Zionist establishment, from weakness or naïveté or by force of habit and ways of thinking acquired in the diaspora, believed that this country could be obtained by amicable means, by gradually buying and settling it. This was a utopian dream, for it naturally had to be taken by force, from both the British and the Arabs.

Jabotinsky realised this elementary fact and made it into one of his fundamental tenets. The anti-British underground movements gave it concrete expression. And then the Zionist establishment, too, was forced or dragged into the same course. ZaHaL, the Israel army was established.

The fundamental ideological-political conception of the FFI, that we are the natural masters of the whole of *Eretz Israel* and that it is our duty to seek its liberation has, however, not yet been fully accepted; hence the political-ethical convolutions and contortions of the State of Israel after the Six Day War. To this day the Israeli army is called ZaHaL, an acronym that stands for "The Israel Defence Forces." The principle of defence inherited from the days of the Haganah, the Jewish self-defence league set up in this country along the lines of similar defence leagues in countries where Jews were subject to pogroms, has been incorporated in the name of Israel's army and become part of the conceptual setting of Israel's leadership.

That this is a political and conceptual error has been amply proven by the course of events, for the functions assumed by this so-called Defence Force are still those of a liberating army re-conquering its homeland and not merely warding off external attack.

In a Jewish state that disposes of a national popular army, however badly misnamed, there is no room for an underground movement of any kind. Yet the fundamental ideological principles of the FFI still stand. Zionism, the State of Israel and its army still constitute a national and territorial liberation movement. In the diaspora all Jewish resources must be directed to defence and protection. In *Eretz Israel* they must be channelled into the war of liberation.

2. Rhapsody — ZaHaL, The Israeli Army

This chapter may also be regarded as an intermezzo, which is not to say that ZaHaL as such is an intermezzo. If we are to continue our musical imagery, ZaHaL is the Eroica of Jewish revival.

The Israeli Army came as a startling revelation to the whole world and not least of all to the Jews themselves. The greatness of the event is perhaps best illustrated by the following highly symbolic, historical coincidence.

Some time in 1953 a remarkable series of ancient letters was discovered in the Judean desert. These were the letters of the last commander of ancient Judea, of Simon Bar Kokhba, the leader of the last great revolt against the Romans and the Patriarch and perhaps also the king of Israel in the years A.D. 132-136. The letters, addressed to commanders in various theatres of operation, were personally signed by him. Now they are on display at the Israel Museum in Jerusalem.

This by itself is an outstanding archaeological discovery. But it is not the most miraculous part of the story. The true miracle lies in the fact that the person who found the letters of the last Jewish commander was the well-known archaeologist, General Yigael Yadin, effectively the first commander of the new Jewish army.

For one thousand eight hundred and twenty years Bar Kokhba's letters lay hidden in the Judean desert, in clay pots where they were preserved for some unknown date in the future. No one had got there in the meantime. No one had touched them, until they were discovered, not haphazardly, but as a result of a thorough exploration of this desert, in a search after the traces left there by our ancestors. They were waiting until they reached their final destination. The letters of Bar Kokhba, the last commander of the Jewish army, thus reached the first commander of the new Jewish army after one thousand eight hundred and twenty years, as if by personal delivery.

This is no poet's fancy—this happened.

There had been Jewish soldiers and fighters in the meantime, as well—after Bar Kokhba and before Yigael Yadin—but the last organized independent Jewish army in ancient days was Bar Kokhba's and the first, organized fighting Jewish army in modern times was that commanded by Yigael Yadin. The letters may have arrived a little late, but they fell into the right hands, delivered from army to army, from commander to commander.

When you come to Jerusalem go to see those letters. You will comprehend their meaning, even if you cannot read them. You will then understand what has happened here, an extraordinary feat verging on the sublime. If you associate this experience with the visionary siting of Herzl's tomb between the Memorial to the holocaust and the military cemetery, perhaps you will no longer look upon the Israeli army as an army like any other. Perhaps you will then understand that anybody who dares talk about Israel's "militarism" is blaspheming against something that is both precious and holy. He is committing an act of profound impiety. After two thousand years of exile, after having experienced genocide in Europe, this is the only people in the world that still has to fight for the right to live as a people in its own homeland. Can there be anything more sacred than the fighting force of this people? But from where does the Jewish people derive the military prowess it has so suddenly manifested? For two thousand years it has been deprived of political independence and of the possibility to develop any military tradition. It had to fall back on the protection of others, and came to rely on their help. Often, Jews looked upon conscription into the armies of other nations as a decree to be averted and evaded. Army life was regarded as a threat to Jewish religion, especially in Czarist Russia where Jewish soldiers were conscripted for 25 years and sent to some remote place where they were totally out of touch with Judaism. Nor did the Jews as a rule look upon these countries as such great benefactors that they should gladly serve in their armies and give their lives for a country where pogroms, discrimination and oppression were commonplace.

In this way arose the image of the cowardly Jew, the Jew who evades military service, who refuses to fight and does not know how to fight.

It is an ironical sidelight that the Arabs used to refer to the Jews as the "sons of death," in contempt for their unwarlike behaviour. European Christians could tell another story, for they knew that Jews feared death least of all, preferring immolation to the betrayal of their faith.

But this is not the whole of the story. There has been also quite a number of Jewish soldiers. In Spain there were Jewish officers and commanders, and in the Polish war of independence Jewish units fought under the leadership of orthodox rabbis. In France, England, Australia and the U.S.A. there had always been Jews known for their courage and military talents. Above all, after the Zionist movement came into being, the fighting forces of the nation began to stir. There were Jewish units fighting in the First World War and a Jewish Brigade in the second, and there were

Jewish fighters in the ghettoes and the underground resistance movements.

Accordingly, the necessary talents—and above all the courage and willingness—never disappeared. In ancient times the Jewish army excelled both in strategy and courage. The Persians set up Jewish military colonies to protect their extensive empire. In the diaspora, however, these aptitudes were submerged, lying hidden away in the depths of the Jewish soul like Bar Kokhba's letters buried in a cave—until the right time would come.

It came, against the background of the horrors of Europe, and the threats of the Arab assassins who had already shown their prowess in the slaughter of women, children and old men in Hebron and Safed and Jerusalem, when acting under British protection.

It seemed that the nation was suddenly gathering all its latent military strength, stirring the embers of its ancient courage and strategic talents which all too often had been wasted on foreign battlefields and revolutions. They were all rekindled in the firm resolution: No more pogroms in the diaspora and certainly no more pogroms in *Eretz Israel*. Never again will the Jewish nation stand by passively, in reliance on a Russian or German or British policeman.

With the same talents and speed with which Yeshiva students had mastered modern physics, Jewish boys mastered fighter planes and modern tanks. The aptitudes had lain dormant, but they were there, to be conjured up by the spirit of "never again." Never again will Massada fall.

This new Jewish fighting spirit and self-reliance came as no little surprise to many gentiles. Perhaps it was General De Gaulle, the staunch Catholic, who best formulated their attitude: "We have always been merciful in our attitude towards the Jews, but they are ungrateful, a domineering nation." De Gaulle, like so many good Christians eager to prove their Christianity by showing mercy to the Jews in spite of the long accounts they had with them, in spite of the Jewish denial or betrayal of Jesus Christ, would no doubt have been willing to extend his compassion to persecuted Jews pleading for grace and forgiveness. But suddenly he was confronted by a new variety of Jews, who do not plead for mercy but want French Mirage aircraft instead, and do not even need French pilots to fly them because they have their own.

Are these really *new* Jews? Certainly not. They are the same Jews, who have merely revived their former spirit, their former being which they were forced to submerge during their period of exile. Outwardly they might have been Shylocks, frightened little Jews, praying for the grace of heaven and appealing to the good gentiles, but inside, in the words of the eternal song, "David the King of Israel was alive." The song refers to David—not to Moses. Moses left his laws and commandments behind him. It was David, the King of Israel, whose untarnished survival was being asserted, because outwardly he no longer appeared to exist: neither his sovereign kingdom nor the great land he had conquered for his people. That is why this song more than any other was chosen to bolster the Jewish sense of security. David's legacy was no substitute for that of Moses and the prophets, for prayers and scholarship and the Jewish way of life, but was kept intact in addition to all these for when the time and the opportunity would be ripe. David more than any other ancient Hebrew king stands for Jewish military prowess, and he is still alive among us.

In the nooks and crannies of history and the Jewish soul, as in the caves of the Judean desert, this force remained latent, but waiting to be recovered. Why it came some ten years too late, what might have happened if ZaHaL had been set up in 1938 rather than in 1948, how many millions could have been saved and would be living here now in a great Davidic commonwealth, is another chapter.

Here we are solely concerned with the fact that there is nothing more sacred than the army of the Jewish people.

Its achievements and strength and its dedication spring from that holy resolution: Never again shall the Jews be led like sheep to the slaughter. Never again shall they live at the mercy of a gentile world, however kindly disposed.

This is the moral driving force behind the Israeli Army, which cannot be equalled because there can be no loftier ideal than the one that inspires it. There can be no cause that is more right and just than the cause of Jewish liberation from a world of evil hypocrisy.

On the first Independence Day after the Six Day War, the military parade marched through the liberated city of Jerusalem, along the walls of the Old City. This was the most beautiful of all the parades that had preceded it. And undoubtedly the author must have suffered from a hallucination when he seemed to discern among the soldiers marching there among the tanks his own brothers who were exterminated in the Janov camp in the Polish city of Lwow—by the Germans or by their lusty henchmen, the Poles, the Ukrainians or the Lithuanians. It was very real, though.

The spectacle itself, however, was no hallucination. Here was a Jewish army marching through the liberated city of Jerusalem, a triumphant army which in six days had defeated forces far superior in number and in arms, and this only twenty-five years after six million of the members of the same nation had been led to slaughter in the furnaces of Auschwitz. Still the same nation. Over there the boys who fought and won in the Six Day War would again have been led to Auschwitz. And those who were led like sheep to the slaughter over there, my brothers and all our brethren, had they been here, had they been led at the right time to fight their own war of liberation, would have fought with the same courage and genius as our boys did and are doing here.

It is the same nation, only in different situations and in different moods. It is the same nation after having lost its illusions about what the gentiles and their cultures are capable of.

3. Caesura

And now we come to that brief, stirring moment in the history of the State of Israel entitled Adolf Eichmann. The Israeli parliament never knew a shorter meeting than that convened by David Ben Gurion, the then prime minister, on the 25th May, 1960, to announce: "I wish to inform the House that some time ago Israeli security services discovered the whereabouts of Adolf Eichmann together with other Nazi leaders who were responsible for what they called 'the final solution of the Jewish problem.' Eichmann is now in Israel awaiting trial under the terms of the Law for the Punishment of Nazis and Nazi Collaborators."

All that happened afterwards—the trial, the shocking testimonies, the slow unwinding of the scroll of the holocaust—how the decision was reached at Wannsee, the stages of the operation and its horrors, the correct bureaucratic behaviour of Eichmann, the reading out of the judgment, and finally his execution by hanging and the dispersion of his ashes over the sea—did not come up to that single moment.

No doubt the Eichmann trial was a historic opportunity to unfold the horrors of the Nazi extermination before the world and our own people. The main significance of the Eichmann affair, however, was that one of the chief persecutors and exterminators of the Jews was being tried and sentenced by the court of a Jewish government in *Eretz Israel*. This was the great triumph of the Jewish nation over its many enemies of whom Eichmann, that arch mediocrity, was merely a personification.

Nobody ever thought of the Eichmann trial in terms of meting out just punishment to a Nazi criminal, though undoubtedly Eichmann was more than a mere bureaucrat carrying out orders from above, as he wished to present himself. It was not a personal affair of Adolf Eichmann, but went much further and much deeper: It embraced the entire Nazi leadership, including all those ideologists, philosophers, artists, writers, historians and intellectuals who had prepared the ground for it; and the entire Nazi party with its vast membership.

Contrary to what some would like to believe, the Nazi regime was not an oligarchic dictatorship imposing its will on the German people. Nazism was a fairly legitimate and legal function of the desire of the German people to achieve world domination. In its anti-Semitic attitudes there can be no question that it represented the feelings of the majority of the German people, whatever their motives. The swastika was a direct descendant of the cross. Though in the absence of the necessary psychological and political conditions the cross did not always assume that crooked shape, it had assiduously sown the seeds of hate and destruction.

Hitler, by his lights, was right in using anti-Semitism as a means for gaining access to and domination over other nations. However much the various European countries, in the east and in the west, may have hated the Germans, they hated the Jews more. Many Frenchmen, Poles, Ukrainians and Lithuanians were willing to forgive Hitler his hostility towards them, provided he would once and for all rid Europe of its Jewish incubus. Without this widespread and deep-rooted hatred Hitler would never have been able to implement his scheme—the only one of his schemes that did prove successful.

It worked only thanks to the active collaboration of other nations and the indifference, or tacit consent of other largely hostile institutions such as the Vatican, the Western democracies and Communism. Many who for various reasons were unable to implement such an extermination programme on their own, rejoiced in their hearts at the fact that others were doing the job for them.

This does not mean that outstanding criminals, both at the planning and at the executive level, should not be brought to trial. That, however, can hardly settle the historic account—if it can ever be settled.

But one item in that account was squared by that brief moment in the Knesset, when the prime minister of the State of Israel announced the capture of Eichmann, and his impending trial in Israel.

Before that there had already been the Nuremberg trials. There, however, the Jewish people were not sitting in judgement over its exterminators. We had quite a few partners there, on the prosecutor's bench. Indeed the communist world, in Poland and in the U.S.S.R., has been trying to obfuscate the Jewish element; Hitler's victims were Poles, Russians, Bulgars, etc., but never Jews. The horrors of Babi Yar are indicative of attempts to continue the extermination by destroying the Jewish dead as well, in the endeavour to wipe the Jewish people off the face of the world. Stalin wanted to do the same for the survivors, but simply did not live long enough.

That moment in Jerusalem was unique because for the first time the Jewish people were the arbiters and judges of their persecutors. Personally, Eichmann was hardly worth the whole show; he might even have derived some pleasure from being able to end his life with all the limelight on him. The recapitulation of the history of the Nazi horrors will no doubt fail to ward off human forgetfulness. The decisive historical aspect was quite a different one: that the reborn State of Israel in the land of the Jews, in Jerusalem, the city of Solomon and David, was finally sitting in trial against a figure that was the living personification of anti-Semitism, the embodiment of the will of many powerful nations, churches, parties and philosophies to put an end to the Jewish people.

The word *"Loesung"*—solution—used by the Germans to designate this scheme lends itself to many connotations by the mere alteration of its prefix. The whole gentile case may be summed up in these variations: You, the Jews, were throughout the ages striving for *Erloesung,* that is, for salvation. In the last century you tried to invade our German (or other) flesh and blood and spirit by means of *Aufloesung,* a process of dissolution, but we could not stomach that, either. We want you neither as a great nation that has found its salvation, nor as a people that has merged with us. We shall therefore carry out an *Endloesung,* a final solution. Thoroughness is a peculiarly German characteristic. Not all other nations would have arrived at such a solution or dared to undertake it. But many, if not all, had their own *Loesungen* or solutions. None of them suggested *Erloesung,* or redemption.

The trial of Eichmann—the symbolic representative of this *Endloesung*—by the Jewish nation in Jerusalem, the capital of Israel, was a resounding historic answer to anti-Semitism in all its varieties and shades; the best possible answer to the desire to deprive us of our existence and revival. Jewish Jerusalem thus served notice on Berlin, the Vatican and the Kremlin—

"The State of Israel which came into being in defiance of your wishes, in Jerusalem, its capital, is sitting in judgment upon the man who symbolises your age-old hatred for our people."

The State of Israel is responsible for the existence, survival and salvation of the Jewish nation, and let this be known by all. This is its destiny and its purpose, the end and be all of its existence.

9

ERETZ ISRAEL OR PALESTINE

HERE we have been talking about Zionism as a Jewish revolution, indulging in historical analyses, while the State of Israel and the world at large are intent on the solution of one specific issue: the Arab-Israel conflict. So far we have been talking almost as if that were a mere side-issue, as if the decisive, real problems could be viewed from a lofty pinnacle, making them dwindle into insignificance.

This is actually so. A considerable, if not a decisive part of the theoretical, political and moral debate derives from the fact that the roots of the problem are ignored, that the conflict is regarded as being between two equal parties, two ordinary countries at loggerheads about some border territories, and trying to settle the dispute by way of conquest or compromise. The singularity of the problem is lost sight of, to no small extent through our own fault. Without all that has been said in the foregoing chapters our approach to the conflict with the "Arab world" remains incomprehensible.

Before we state our position we have to interpose another prefatory chapter on the concept *Eretz Israel,* whose English translation is "Land of Israel." We prefer not to use this translation because of the pitfalls it contains which are partly responsible for the prevailing confusion of issues.

Prior to 1948, when people spoke about the Land of Israel, they were simply referring to the original Hebrew name of Palestine or what Christians call the Holy Land. Israel until 1948 meant "people of Israel" and was synonymous with the Jewish people. This is not the place to discuss the different names by which this nation has been known in history—Judea, Israel, Hebrews. At any rate, until 1948 the reference was clear: Israel meant only one thing, the people of Israel or the Jewish people. In some circles it was customary to talk about Israelites without even thinking that the term had any territorial connotations. On the contrary, it was taken to refer to "members of the Mosaic faith," Jews by confession only.

When speaking about the Land of Israel people thus clearly referred to the land of the Jews and obviously the term comprised the entire country and not any part or section of it.

The term Holy Land was used to stress the religious significance of that country. Palestine was a purely geographical term without any national or demographic implications.

In 1948, the Jewish State, set up in a small portion of the geographic region called Palestine, was given the name Israel. Whether the choice was appropriate or not is irrelevant. What is relevant, however, is that a name by itself cannot create a new reality or substance, nor can it alter or erase a former one. The name *Land of Israel,* the land of the Jews, applied to this country in the past even when there were but few Jews living in it. That there were so few Jews in the country was not for lack of desire on their part to live there, but was, rather, due to expulsion and persecution. There is no justification whatsoever for all of a sudden assigning the name *Land of Israel* only to that part of it which was liberated in 1948 and not to all those parts which, through our fault or incapacity, were not liberated at that time. The name Palestine never ceased to connote the entire country.

A foolish attempt was also made to refer to the Israelis, the residents of the State of Israel, as members of a new nation not identical with the Jewish people.

Both attempts—to change a geographic, historic concept

and a national, historic concept—have failed. No separate Israeli nation, distinct from the rest of the Jewish nation, has emerged. In 1948 there were about 700,000 Israelis. Now there are 3,000,000. The pressure of the Russian Jews and the constant flow of immigration from other countries has torpedoed any attempt to create a separatist Israeli nation within the 1948 borders of the State of Israel.

The Six Day War dealt a death blow to any attempt to apply the name "Israel" to the territories of the State of Israel alone. Even those who now advocate the idea of withdrawal from certain areas in exchange for peace, talk about withdrawal from the territories of *Eretz Israel,* that is territories that form part of the Jewish homeland. Once it is resolved—or it transpires—that there will be no withdrawal from these territories, it will certainly not be *Eretz Israel* that has expanded: At most, one might say that the State of Israel has annexed additional areas of *Eretz Israel.*

Our purpose in calling this chapter *Eretz Israel* was precisely to eliminate the error that has been invading many people's minds since 1948 regarding the meaning of the *Land of Israel.* People forgot that Israel meant a nation, the Jewish nation, and only thought of it as a state. Hence the *Land of Israel* began to sound like the territory of the State of Israel. Consequently it appeared to them that additional alien territories were being seized or conquered.

Constant immigration and of late also the renewed impetus of Russian Jewry have so far prevented the State of Israel from adopting a policy of national segregation. It was thus constantly borne in upon everybody that *the State of Israel is the only country in the world which was established not only for its own citizens, but for a nation most of which is still outside its territories.*

The people of Israel, the Jewish nation, is exerting pressure on the State of Israel to prevent its de-historisation and de-naturation. They will not allow it to abandon its mission as the home of the entire Jewish people. For a long time *Eretz Israel,* on the other hand, had exerted no overt pressure on the State of Israel so that here there was a danger of de-historisation and de-naturation and of narrow confinement. This danger was averted by the Six Day War which broke down the previous artificial, fictitious boundaries. This event cannot be ascribed solely to the good offices of our Arab enemies who tried to liquidate the State of Israel. It came about by virtue of a latent, internal logic and justice which continues to operate at a deeper stratum of Jewish history.

The State of Israel in its pre-1967 borders not only lacked the necessary strategic depth and the minimum space for economic development, but it also made no historical sense whatever. Historically, *Eretz Israel* was forged into a national-political unit solely by the Jewish people and by no other.

In stating this fact—which can be contradicted only through ignorance or vicious falsification—the metaphysical-religious aspect of this being the land promised to the descendants of Abraham, Isaac and Jacob is deliberately ignored. We mention this aspect only because most of those who are at present taking an interest in the Middle East beyond the direct interest generated by oil and military bases—the Islamic and the Christian world—fully acknowledge this religious-metaphysical aspect. Nevertheless we intend to explore the question on its purely historical, non-metaphysical merits.

It is a historical fact that before the people of Israel came to this country it was not a political factor. It was split up into numerous city states held by different tribes. Canaan or Rethno, the Egyptian parallel, was merely geographic rather than a political or national concept. Though a material civilization may have flourished in these city states, there was no national or political cohesion, nor has any Canaanite language been preserved. It was only when the tribes of Israel came in the 13th century B.C. that a national political entity, a single commonwealth was set up with one language, one culture and one religion—that was to become a national religion despite its universal aspects. In this country the nation experienced many political vicissitudes. During the rule of David and Solomon its domains expanded tremendously. At other times, internal dissensions and divisions hampered its political life. Destruction was followed by revival (586-536 B.C.). Periods of war alternated with periods of peace, periods of expansion with periods of contraction. There were times when it enjoyed full sovereignty and others when its independence was curtailed. Throughout, however, for a period of 1400 years, until after the Bar Kokhba revolt, the country was undoubtedly *Eretz Israel*—inhabited by one people for whom it was the only homeland. Here this people created most of its cultural assets, many of which have been transmitted to the world at large through the medium of religion. Its geopolitical position, on the crossroads between three continents, wedged in first between the ancient Egyptian empire and the Asian empires of Assyria and Babylon, and then between East and West—Greece and Rome on the one hand and the Persians and the Parthians on the other—was both a blessing and a curse. This made it a target for conquest, but also reinforced the nation's self-sufficiency and self-reliance, and taught it to absorb outside influences without being submerged by them, and to fight for its political no less than for its spiritual independence. Kings, prophets and others who fought for the nation's freedom, (such as the Maccabees), who were both its makers and its sons, imbued the Jewish population filling the country's towns and villages, its valleys and hills, with that deep-rooted, cohesive sense of national unity and that unique patriotism that was to give this country its special value and sanctity. Partly transmitted to the entire civilized world, essentially it always remained the prerogative of one nation—the Jewish people.

There is no precedent in human history of such an intimate relationship between people and country. Leaving aside the religious element of this being the land promised to our forefathers who came there on the strength of this promise they believed in, there still remains also the non-metaphysical or physical fact that after the destruction of the Temple, the symbol of its political and spiritual independence, the nation continued to live in this land for centuries and to fight for its freedom. After the final expulsion, when the people of Israel had been dispersed over the face of the globe, it still did not cease to regard this as its sole homeland, confident in its ultimate return for a new era of creation and freedom in a reborn Jewish commonwealth.

Jews never ceased to mention the return to their land in their prayers. The Scriptures they never tired of reading and studying enhanced their awareness that *Eretz Israel* is their true homeland. Faith in the Messiah implied the return to Zion; and Jewish history is interspersed with many a Messianic movement. Jewish pilgrims kept flocking to the Land of Israel. Soil from *Eretz Israel* was carried overseas to be interred with the dead in the diaspora. *"Next year in Jerusalem"* was what Jews wished each other on the most important holidays: Seder Eve—the beginning of Passover, and Yom Hakippurim—the Day of Atonement.

All this, you might say, indicates "only" their religious attachment. But no. When the Zionist movement was founded many of its leaders were non-believers. They were neither religious nor observant. Their ideas rested on a purely secular basis. Yet they called their movement after the ancient Zion, the name that stands for *Eretz Israel* in the mind of every Jew. When Herzl tried to set up a state in Uganda for the persecuted Jewish masses of Russia, he solemnly declared that he intended it only as a provisional refuge because the ultimate homeland can be only *Eretz Israel*. Also those Zionists who were confirmed socialists and atheists regarded this as their national homeland, and none other.

This is a unique historical phenomenon, no less miraculous than the survival of the Jewish people in and despite the diaspora. Evidently the two are interrelated. One of the reasons for the nation's survival in the diaspora, with persecution on the one hand and the temptations of conversion and assimilation on the other, was its loyalty to this homeland which it knew was standing in wait for it.

For the land did stand there, waiting to be resettled by its rightful owners. This again is not metaphysics but a historical fact. Just as *Eretz Israel* had never been a single national territory before the arrival of the people of Israel, it never again became such once that people had been exiled from it. No nation regarded it as its homeland; no population that ever lived here developed into a nation: No sovereign, independent state was ever set up here, from the time the Jewish commonwealth was destroyed until the Jewish people's recent return. This country made us a people; our people made this country. No other people in the world made this country; this country made no other people in the world. Now again we are beginning to make this country and again this country is beginning to make us.

Wars were waged over it, but not for its own sake. The goal was either to control the Christian holy places or the strategic positions it offered as a passageway to other coveted targets. Never was a war of national liberation fought here by any except the Jews.

The Crusader kingdom—which never was a national state but consisted of a series of forts and trading outposts manned by adventurers and religious fanatics from many lands—was so short-lived precisely because it lacked any national-political interest in this country. The Christians who had come to redeem the Holy Sepulchre or to find new markets in the East and new trade routes to Europe (one of the ulterior, non-religious motives of the Crusades) were indeed willing to make the pilgrimage, but never to turn the country into their national homeland.

Islam fought over it in order to drive out the Christian infidels but never dreamt of establishing any separate national-political entity there. In Islamic days the country was alternately ruled by Egypt, Baghdad, Damascus and Constantinople.* "There is no such thing as Palestine in history, absolutely not," said Dr. Hitti, the renowned Arab historian, speaking about Arab history, of course. Administratively it was considered part of Syria, harking back to Roman days, when it was given the name *Palaestina,* or more precisely *Syria Palaestina.*

Nobody knows any longer just why this peculiar name was chosen, but the exact date when this was done is known: after the Bar Kokhba rising. The reason, too, is known: to erase any connection with the Jewish people and help the world forget their primary title to it. Before the revolt the Roman name for it was *Judea.*

What is so peculiar about the name Palaestina? That it was a totally anachronistic neologism coined from an archaism. The name of a long-forgotten people, if ever it was such, which was living on the southern coast of *Eretz Israel* and tried to push its way inland at the time the tribes of Israel were settling there on their journey from the East, it was revived for this purpose. The invasion was halted in Davidic times, though for several centuries the Philistines held on to a narrow coastal strip near Ashkelon. In the period of the Second Temple they were completely assimilated into Middle Eastern-Hellenistic culture. In fact they originally hailed from the Greek islands, and it is mooted that the name might have been a Greek inspiration. It was obviously a ridiculous act of hate and vengeance to call the entire country after those forgotten tribes who had never made it their own, and had never achieved political independence or created any original culture there. Who has ever heard of a Philistine language, a Philistine religion, a Philistine culture

---

*The centre of Islam moved from place to place—Baghdad, Damascus, Cairo, Constantinople, but never Jerusalem.

or a Philistine literature—except in another, much later and equally corrupt sense! Apart from a few potsherds of vessels modelled after the Greek fashion, the name is all that is left of them—a name whose entire function was to obliterate the true historical name and the true cultural significance of this country: *Eretz Israel.*

The change of name did not achieve its purpose. Ironically enough, it is now again being bandied about with similar malevolent intent. All it ever became was a geographical term, serving as a substitute for the ancient national names *Eretz Israel,* or Israel and Judea—or as a parallel for the religious term, the *Holy Land.*

Since this other name, the Holy Land, is also being misused, it likewise deserves to be examined. Certain places in this country are sacred to Christianity. This is only reasonable, considering that this religion had its birth in this country and that all its fundamental myths are based on certain events, above all events associated with the life and death of its founder that are presumed to have taken place here. This, however, has nothing to do with any national or political affiliation with this country.

Islam, too, has a holy place here, though of much smaller significance to this religion than are the sites sacred to Christianity (and on a flimsier basis), since it is not related to the inception of that religion. The holiness of this place to Islam derives solely from the legend that Muhammad, after a miraculous night flight from Arabia to Jerusalem, ascended from there to heaven. Islam was born in the Arabian peninsula. Why then was it necessary to have Muhammad ascend to heaven precisely from the Temple Mount in Jerusalem, the site of the Jewish Temple? We shall not go into questions of theology and mythology or enter into arguments with either Christianity or Islam. Suffice it to note that Burma, for instance, is a Buddhist country, but on these grounds advances no claims to India, the birthplace of Buddha.

Initially there were some attempts to turn the Arab war

against the Jews in *Eretz Israel* into a kind of *jihad*, a holy war, like the early Islamic campaigns whose object was to impose the Islamic faith upon the world, or like some of their warfare against the Crusaders. These attempts, however, soon failed. There are Moslem countries which have no political interest whatsoever in fighting for *Eretz Israel*. And at the same time there are Christian Arabs who violently oppose Zionism and the State of Israel.

Generally, religious wars have gone somewhat out of fashion. They no longer fit into this modern day and age. Moreover, unlike Christianity in Crusader times, Zionism never invoked the religious motive but was based on the national rights and needs of the Jewish people. In Judaism, religion and nationality are closely interwoven into a single fabric, and *Eretz Israel* is the Holy Land for every believing Jew. As distinct from Christianity or Islam, however, *Eretz Israel* is holy to Judaism not only because of any special places or special events connected with it: It is the entire land that is holy, as the land of our forefathers and the sole future haven of our nation.

Hence any talk about "the land holy to all religions" is, as a political argument, either a piece of ignorance or of demagoguery. There can be no comparison between the sacredness of *Eretz Israel* to Christianity and Islam, and its sanctity to the Jewish nation as a homeland.

Let us now go back to that geographical designation which was invented after the destruction of the Jewish commonwealth some 1800 years ago to mark the total severance of the Jews from their land. Having failed in its purpose and having been relegated to the status of a geographical name, it is now trying to usurp a new national significance, with the same object of preventing the Jewish people from regaining its independence in this land. The name *Palestine* assumed political significance with the Balfour Declaration and the League of Nations mandate, when it became necessary to define the area to which the international recognition of the political rights of the Jewish nation should apply. The area to which the name *Palestine* was thus applied included both banks of the Jordan, although the northern and eastern borders were artificially drawn according to a geometric pattern by a random division between the spheres of influence of British and French imperialism. In the south, too, the border then fixed was not a matter of historical tradition but the result of a dispute between Turkey and Egypt that was resolved through the intervention of the British empire at the beginning of the 20th century. It was neither a natural nor an ethnic border, the Negev and the Sinai peninsula geographically and otherwise constituting a single unit.

In the Balfour Declaration and the mandate of the League of Nations the name Palestine thus referred to a considerable portion of the historic *Eretz Israel*, as was clearly understood both by Great Britain and the nations that ratified the mandate in July 1922. In September of that year, however, after an abortive British attempt to make a member of the vassal Hashemite dynasty the ruler of Damascus, the Hedjaz sheiks were given Trans-Jordan instead, to compensate them for the loss of the Syrian territory previously promised to them. Subsequently the name *Palestine—Eretz Israel* was (under the Mandate) applied only to the western bank of the Jordan.

After the East bank of the Jordan had thus been arbitrarily cut off from the West Bank, Zionism nevertheless did not rescind its title to *Eretz Israel* on the other bank of the Jordan as well. The Zionist authorities negotiated with the Hashemite Emir Abdulla for the purchase of extensive lands there, and the deal fell through only because of the premature publicity it received. Needless to say, orthodox Judaism continued to adhere to the Biblically promised borders "from the Euphrates to the River of Egypt," now the Suez Canal.

In mandatory times, moreover, the entire population of

this country, Jews and Arabs alike, was referred to as Palestinian. Some still keep in their drawers old passports and identity cards issued by the government of *Palestine-Eretz-Israel* in this fashion.

The mission of Zionism, as a national liberation movement, was once again to turn *Palaestina* into *Eretz Israel*, to reverse the decree of the Roman empire which had tried to change history by a change of name. Both heaven and earth decreed otherwise. The letters of Bar Kokhba, the last Jewish commander quashed by the Romans, fell into the hands of Yigael Yadin, and *Palestine* is once again becoming *Eretz Israel*. The Jewish nation, like Bar Kokhba's letters were both safely stowed away to re-emerge intact when the time came: *Eretz Israel* lay hidden deep inside the heart of every Jew in the diaspora.

Not only the letters were waiting to be found by a Jewish soldier. The entire land lay waiting. Herzl, seventy years ago, put it in very simple words: *"Give the nation without a land the land that is without a nation."* The landless nation had given proof, through its faithfulness and its refusal to assimilate, that it was waiting for the right historical moment to return to its land: *Eretz Israel,* and no other. But the land, too, by never having been throughout 1800 years a distinct national and political entity, had proved that it was waiting for the nation. The very soil, which lay waste and idle, was waiting for its loyal sons to redeem its barrenness.

Why the nation and the land had needed so long to be reunited cannot be analysed here. Internal and external, national as well as international causes were responsible for this delay.

That the State of Israel was set up in only part of *Eretz Israel* may have been a direct outcome of the fact that only part of the nation had realised the greatness and urgency of the Zionist cause. The consent grudgingly given in the past to various partition schemes never constituted an admission that the Jewish nation had ceded its title to the whole of *Eretz Israel* or given up its claim to it. According to those who gave their consent—and there were always those who withheld theirs—they were swayed by reasons of expediency or necessity. To the extent that their consent was prompted by the belief that independence was essential in order to repatriate the Jews of the diaspora, they were right. To the extent that they thought partition would lead to peace with the Arabs, the pretenders to the title for *Ezetz Israel,* they were wrong. To the extent they thought the establishment of a state in part of the country implied the final implementation of the Zionist idea, they were wrong. To the extent they thought, even unconsciously, that the state would merely provide a new, more efficient and militant means for the attainment of the Zionist ideal—the return of the entire nation still in the diaspora to *Eretz Israel* and the restoration of that part of *Eretz Israel* that was still in foreign hands to the nation—they were perfectly right.

The establishment of the State of Israel in 1948 was not the end of the road, neither for the nation nor for the country. The reconversion of *Palaestina* into *Eretz Israel* is continuing.

10

THE ARAB-JEWISH CONFLICT

JUST as in the *Land of Israel,* the word "Israel" is often wrongly applied to the State of Israel rather than to the Jewish people, the term Arab-Israeli Conflict becomes misleading when it is taken to mean a conflict between neighbouring countries—the Arab states and the State of Israel. The misconception inherent in this view gives rise to charges of Israel having occupied her neighbours' territories—which of course is not done in this modern, pacifist, moral world where the territorial integrity of one's neighbours is always respected. And this misconception with regard to the conflict also breeds irrelevant compromise solutions based on territorial concessions.

This entire line of argument stems from a superficial, fragmented view of what is going on here. The Middle East Conflict would be a much better term, because it right away indicates that this is not a conflict between two rival states about this or the other piece of land, but that it is a question of a fundamental change in the map of the Middle East.

The conflict did not start with the Six Day War in 1967. Nor did it start in 1948 with the establishment of the State of Israel. Neither was it precipitated by the U.N. partition resolution of 1947. These three events were all stages in a much deeper conflict, none of them final. Politicians are fully entitled to solve problems by pragmatic means, as long as they realise the nature of the problems they are dealing with. They must define for themselves whether they are handling a political or economic problem, or whether they have been called in to resolve a deep-seated, historical issue. Though politics may occasionally make history, sometimes, and perhaps more often—ours being a classical case in point—it is history that makes politics. Any politician—or any other person, young or old—who out of impatience or impotence decides to throw history to the winds and be instead practical and pragmatic is really doing nothing of the sort. He is merely whistling against the wind.

Those who had been seeking pragmatic, stop-gap solutions to Nazi imperialism were responsible for the disaster of the Second World War. Those who sought pragmatic, stop-gap solutions to the problems of the Jews in Europe were directly responsible for their annihilation. All the various partition plans of *Eretz Israel,* offered as pragmatic, stop-gap solutions, merely led to renewed warfare.

Had Zionism been accomplished in a revolutionary outburst right after the Second World War, neither the artifical Kingdom of Jordan, nor Palestinian Arab nationalism would ever have seen the light of this world. In line with her former practice, Egypt would not have intervened, being in the throes of her own war of liberation. The idea of an Egyptian empire, inspired by Nasser's megalomania, would probably never have been spawned. Under the Weizmann-Feisal agreement, Saudia had already given full consent to Zionism. The only Arab *state* at loggerheads with Zionism at that time was Syria.

This was no accident, nor was it the result of Syrian extremism, just as Syria's subsequent extremist anti-Israeli attitude was no accident. This attitude has been maintained throughout, no matter how many times the government may have changed hands. Since Roman times *Eretz Israel* has, for purposes of de-Judaization, beeen defined as "south Syria." Consequently Syria, in her imperialist struggle for predominance in the Islamic world, could not countenance the establishment of a separate state in *Eretz Israel,* especially not a Jewish state.

It was therefore no accident that the first anti-Zionist meeting of Arab leaders was convened in 1918 in Damascus, and that for many years anti-Jewish riots in this country were instigated by Syria.

When Egypt decided to oppose the establishment of a Jewish state in *Eretz Israel,* she did so in order to prevent either Iraq or Syria from gaining a foothold here or, as subsequently happened in Nasser's time, in order to quash a nascent, political, non-Arab and non-Moslem factor that might interfere with his dream of ruling over an immense Moslem-Arab empire.

Neither Iraq nor Syria nor Egypt were ever interested in the local Arab population of this country. They coveted the territory as such, not because of any historic or national considerations, but out of sheer greed.

When the Arabs first formed a national movement in opposition to the Ottoman Empire, Palestinians took no part in it. No one considered them as an ethnic or national group, and certainly not as a political factor. The Balfour Declaration was issued on the condition ". . . it being clearly understood that nothing shall be done which may prejudice the civil and religious rights of existing non-Jewish communities in Palestine." In this declaration, which was the most moderate version—from the Jewish point of view—of the many texts proposed, the term Arab was never mentioned, and there was certainly no reference to *Palestinians.* Nor does it speak of political and national rights, but only of civil and religious rights which are accorded as a matter of course in any modern democratic society. This Declaration was approved by fifty-two countries, including the United States, and until September 1922 it also applied to the East bank of the Jordan as an integral part of *Eretz Israel* or *Palestine.*

It was only later, at the instigation of Syrian nationalists and partly in furtherance of the private ambitions of resident aristocratic families (the Husseinis and Nashashibis) that any local opposition to the Zionist cause began. As a rule, this took the form of pogroms—attacks on peaceful villages and religious urban neighbourhoods (Hebron, Safed) which had no stake in Zionism. Women, children and feeble old men were slaughtered in the most barbaric and cowardly fashion, without any semblance of a battle. Marauding gangs were organized, consisting partly of fanatics and partly of professional highway robbers.

During the twenties these activities had the active support of the U.S.S.R., as part of its anti-imperialist programme and the anti-Zionist line adopted according to Marxist doctrine, as well as for reasons of internal politics. In the thirties the initiative passed into the hands of the Nazis. The leader of the nationalist Arab movement was given a post at Nazi Headquarters in Berlin where he also took part in elaborating the Jewish genocide programme. Recent reliable sources reveal that even the notorious Himmler was prepared to release many Jewish children from Germany, but the Grand Mufti Hussein prevented him, and the children were sent to their deaths.

The Arabic nationalist movement was borne by a tiny minority. Most of the local Arab population enjoyed an unprecedented economic boom as a result of the influx of Jewish capital and brainpower. Moreover, no less than 30 per cent of the urban Arab population arrived only then from other Arab territories to profit from the prosperity brought by the "Yahud." (Previous waves of Arab immigration had occurred when Baron Rothschild began developing Jewish colonies at the end of the 19th century; others came to the rural areas that were being developed and made habitable by Jewish pioneers, so that the indigenous Arab population formed a small minority.)

Arab terrorism that was started in 1936 soon degenerated into anti-Arab terrorism. Thousands of Arabs were murdered because they refused to collaborate. Totally devoid of any national consciousness, they were only too willing to live in peace and go about their private business like their forefathers who had never dreamt of nationhood or independence. Had it hinged on the indigenous Arab population, had they been asked for their opinion, there would never have been any fighting. The country would gradually have reverted to its former owners, with a small Arab minority living peacefully, and with equal rights, side by side with the Jews.

Had Zionism followed its original revolutionary course . . . this unfortunately must be a constant refrain. Had a Jewish state been established immediately in the whole of *Eretz Israel*, had millions of Jews been settled there right away, according to Herzl's vision and Nordau's and Jabotinsky's repeated exhortations (and warranted by the plight of the diaspora), the Arabs of this country would never have evolved any national movement, and certainly no separatist Palestinian consciousness.

The lack of resolution on the part of Zionism and the vaccilation of the British thus slowed down the Judaisation of the country and stepped up Arab opposition. Each wave of rioting by the Arabs caused new restrictions to be imposed on the Jewish National Home, inspiring the Arabs to new hopes of being able to put an end to Zionism.

There was no dearth of compromise proposals on the part of the Zionists, including proposals to waive the idea of Jewish independence; or to restrict the proportion of Jews in advance to 40 per cent of the total population; or, in the Mapam version, to set up a bi-national state.

All these developments took place long before the Jewish army had come into being. Contrary to what is commonly thought, therefore, it certainly was not the State of Israel, and quite definitely not its expansion, that aroused the fury of the Arabs, or fostered Arab nationalism, or set fire to the Middle East. The provocation was in the very act of our return to this country; just as the very existence of the Jewish people in the diaspora has been a provocation for many gentiles and a cause for the smouldering hatred that flared up periodically. Contrary to the views of the so-called moderate, compromising Zionists, it has always transpired, as should have been clear from the outset and is becoming more and more evident all the time, this is no war between the State of Israel and the Arabs about such negotiable issues as territories or refugees. It is a war the Arabs are waging against Zionism as such, in any shape or form. On the premise that there can no longer be any Judaism without Zionism—as has been shown by recent developments both in the Jewish and the gentile world—it is a war between the Arabs and the Jewish people. For Zionism of course aims at the complete return of the Jewish people to *Eretz Israel*. This, we must admit, the Arabs have understood better than many semi-Zionists. For there can be no half-way measures here. Zionism means a full return to Zion, and nothing less.

Had it not been for Zionism and the return of the Jews to their homeland, no independent state would have arisen here. This country would have become a prey to constant warfare between various Arab states—Syria, Iraq and Egypt. Saudi Arabia would no doubt also have stepped in to obtain part of the east bank of the Jordan, her northern border. There were no historic, ethnic, linguistic, religious elements, no past tradition, no present consciousness that warranted or prompted the establishment of a Palestinian nation. The Arabs in this country were an offshoot of the nomads from the Arabian desert, who had come here with the Islamic conquest. No doubt some of the former non-Arab inhabitants were converted to Islam, voluntarily or at the point of a sword, in line with the traditional battle cry of militant Islam, "Din Muhammad bissef"—"The Religion of Muhammad—by the Sword."

Even during the period of Arab rule, when *Eretz Israel*

was part of the empires of Baghdad or Damascus, the new town of Ramle served as the administrative centre, never Jerusalem. No pilgrimages were instituted to Jerusalem, like the *hejira* to Mecca. In the 19th century, from 1840 onwards, the Jews formed the absolute majority in Jerusalem. The local Arabs made no attempt to limit their numbers, nor was the alarm sounded in any of the Arab capitals. It is true that the Arabs were inimical to Zionism practically right from the start, but not in the name of any Palestinian nation.

Their objections stemmed solely from dynastic and imperialist interests. The Palestinian nation that is being so greatly publicised now is a totally new product, partly manufactured by Jews. Certain Zionist elements still harboured some of their diaspora-bred cosmopolitan illusions and internationalist dreams. For them Zionism was not a self-supporting ideal, a beautiful vision that needed no further adornment. For them it was a kind of historical accident. Their primary object had been to assimilate, to become part of the liberal or Communist world, but since that world had rejected them, the swing of the pendulum carried them back to their own nation and to this country. But they were still tagging along the fragments of their former, shipwrecked ideologies, as well as the inherent Jewish sense of justice, the ancient Joseph complex, which having failed among the gentiles in Europe, they tried to give full rein to in this country.

Many of the Zionist ideologists thus lulled themselves into the pleasant illusion that the Jewish state would not arise in the same fashion as all other states before it had done—by a war of conquest or liberation. It would come into being in idyllic, pastoral fashion, in love and peace, with song and plough. Moreover, we would bestow this message of love, peace and happiness not only upon ourselves but upon all the inhabitants of this land and the entire Middle East.

It was a beautiful dream indeed. Unfortunately however, it was less realistic and more mystical than any of the messianic visions and experiments of the preceding 2000 years. It was the mysticism of the pure in heart, but simple of mind. It is certainly good to help others, provided those others want your help. There also can be no doubt that ultimately a Jewish state will also be a blessing for the entire Middle East. Indirectly—or dialectically—it is already proving to be a boon to this part of the world, but that was not the reason for our coming here. Ours was a national, egoistic reason. And if there is any nation in the world which has the right to be selfish it is the Jewish nation, which has already paid much too dear a price for its unselfishness, its willingness to give up its existence, and to save other nations and groups.

Nevertheless the Joseph complex persisted. To this day it finds expression in Israel's apologetic, defensive stance, in her constant attempts to prove to the world that she is not the aggressor, leaving the offensive to others and depriving herself of this option. The Arab nations and organizations constantly proclaim their bellicosity. They are proud to be the aggressors, and it does not seem to do them any harm. The Jews, on the other hand, partly as a result of their emancipationary complexes, their desire to appear in a favourable light and thus gain recognition and acclaim, and because of their inherent mentality, are truly unwilling to launch a war of conquest for the liberation of their land.

These organizational and organic elements are the ones who are nowadays seeking to justify the existence of the State of Israel and its enforced expansion by recognizing the rights of the "Palestinian" Arabs.

You will note that it is not a question of recognizing the rights of the Arabs to live as citizens of the State of Israel, but of recognizing the national rights of the Palestinian Arabs —rights they were never deprived of because they never had them. We never destroyed any Arab state because there never was an Arab state here. Even on the remote assumption that had it not been for us, such a state might have arisen here (and the assumption is very remote since it is unlikely that the other Arab states would have countenanced it, nor did the local Arabs have the necessary drive and internal organisation to bring it into being) we would still have been entitled to say: "Sorry, you missed the boat. Now we are here and we won't budge. If you tempt us we might move forward. Never back!"

For we did not come here as colonialists. We came neither like the British imperialists, nor like the French colons in Algeria, nor like the English and Dutch settlers in South Africa. We did not come like emigrants seeking a new continent, a new homeland. We came back home, as the inhabitants of a country who had been driven away from it by force. We were willing to settle in peace, to purchase lands—as we did—from those who happened to be holding them, to reclaim waste lands and deserts. You compelled us to use force. Nor did we drive you out. You ran away, at the instigation of your leaders, through your own folly, and through your own lack of real roots in this land which is not your home. Had the Arab leaders, your own brothers, allowed you to settle in their countries, your true home, the problem of your refugees would have been settled long ago, just as the problem of our refugees has been settled. We did not let our Jewish brethren vegetate in refugee camps.

But in spite of all our trials and tribulations in this country, not just since 1948 but since 1920 when the Arabs had themselves their first pogrom in Jerusalem, there still are Jews who are harrowed by a sense of guilt or indulge in illusions that recognition of the political rights of some fictitious Palestinian nation could provide the solution.

I have generally avoided citing references in this book, because I did not want it to grow into a heavy tome. Here, however I am departing from my practice because the quotation I wish to cite is very recent and is typical of a fairly current historical fallacy used to some advantage in present propaganda. It is all the more interesting because the statement was made by an American Jew and has a good chance of being accepted—probably in all innocence—by the American public.

The Fall 1970 issue of *Forum*, the journal of Columbia University, contained an article by a certain Dr. Arthur Herzberg whom the editors designate as a leading Zionist. Under the title "Palestine—The Logic of Partition Today," he advances the following thesis . . .

> Because I am a Zionist, it is proper that I begin with my own camp. Israel's leading politicians have said repeatedly that there is not, and never has been, a Palestinian Arab nation, and that insofar as the Arabs of Palestine even felt themselves to be part of some larger identity, it was that of being Arab, and not Palestinian. The trouble with this argument is that it evades the facts both of history and of the present. Israeli politicians know that all the modern nationalisms, including their own, arose relatively recently, no earlier than the nineteenth century in Europe and later still in Asia and in Africa. To deny the existence now of a Palestinian Arab national consciousness because it did not exist as such in 1917 is a delusion.

This is no leading Zionist. If he is a Zionist at all, he is a highly misleading one. He also is a very dubious historian if he can draw an analogy of this kind between the Jewish and the "Palestinian" nations. It is a horrible dictum, showing profound ignorance of Zionism in general and Jewish history in particular, of Arab culture and developments in the Arab world, and beyond that, of the very concept of nationality.

The Jewish nation has been in existence for close to 4,000 years. It is returning to its homeland through Zionism which is merely a modern political tool for implementing the urge to return, deeply imbedded within this nation's consciousness. The Jewish nation—as this gentleman who pretends to be a Zionist and a historian had better note—was not born in the 19th century. It was in the 19th century that it came close to extinction, from which it was saved by Zionism. No Palestinian nation has ever existed and it is doubtful whether such a nation will ever arise. The Jewish nation has a birth certificate, a matriculation certificate as well as an identity card, signed by Abraham and Isaac and Jacob, by Moses and David and all the prophets down to Maimonides and Yehuda Halevy and the most recent Jewish geniuses. It has crossed an ocean of blood to preserve its own identity, its creative spirit and full national consciousness.

Can this rich national existence be compared with the Palestinian nation? Who is that nation? What is it? Where and when was it born? What is its identity? What are its distinctive features—physical and mental? And except for the feats of its marauding gangs, what has it ever been known for?

If this is its homeland—why did it never fight for it? Few only seem to be aware of the fact that in all the wars fought against Israel, the combatants were the armies of the neighbouring Arab states, while the million and a half so-called Palestinian Arabs hardly lifted a finger—even when the Jews were in the minority. All they ever did was to roam the countryside, banding together in murderous gangs; and even then they called in outsiders—Kaukaji and others—to act as leaders and reinforcements. Their whole prowess was in murdering old men and children, like the brave "guerillas" who are now throwing bombs in supermarkets, cafeterias and bus stations.

What kind of nation is this that deserts whole cities—Lydda, Ramle, Jaffa—and simply runs away?

But the thesis of the Palestinian nation and its rights is

nevertheless finding supporters throughout the world. It is particularly invidious when it is brought forward by someone who poses both as a Zionist and as a historian.

So much for the absurdity of the analogy between Jewish nationhood and Palestinian nationhood. Now for a few words about Zionism in its confrontation with this animal that calls itself a Palestinian nation.

Let us assume that it does exist. So what? In our firm belief in the justice of our own liberation movement and the imperative need it fills for our own nation, we can but repeat what was said to me by one of the nationalist Arab leaders at our encounter in the central gaol of Jerusalem in 1944: *"After the British have been driven off we shall fight it out between us, and whoever wins—the country shall be his."* Even he, whose claim to this country was admittedly smaller and of more recent origin, never conceded the possibility of "dividing the country between two nations."

11

BEFORE ANY COURT OF JUSTICE

HAD I been asked to decide in a dispute of this kind, as an impartial referee—neither Arab nor Jew, with no prejudices or preconceived feelings towards either side and no personal interest whatsoever—what would I have said after hearing the arguments of the parties?

I would say to the Jew:

You once had in Jerusalem a great and wise king; Solomon was his name. And two women came before him, one with a live infant and another with a dead infant, each claiming that the live child was hers. The king ordered that the live child be divided in two. One of the women agreed, and the other objected. And the wise king said, "The woman who agreed to have the live child cut in half is not his true mother." Indeed, your king was a wise man. Wiser than you.

But there is also a different line of argument that we might adopt, equally true and just, and perhaps still more convincing. Had there indeed been a true court of justice in the world, genuinely disinterested and endowed with that spirit of ultimate justice represented by Nathan the Prophet when he chided King David for taking the lamb of the poor, and by Elijah the Prophet in reprimanding King Ahab, "Hast thou murdered and also taken the inheritance?"— had there been such a court, our plea before it should be as follows:

This is no conflict between two nations, Palestinians and Israelis. First of all, we deny the true existence of a

Palestinian nation. There never has been such a nation. Neither we nor anyone else ever heard about it. There had never been a state in this country, before we came, and its inhabitants never put forward any national claims whatsoever. At most they regarded themselves part of the Arab nation or race, one tiny offshoot of it, a little finger of the huge body squatting over the entire Middle East. Perhaps a nation of this kind might arise here one day, but for the time being there is none. At any rate there can be no juxtaposition between us as two nations.

Secondly, there also is no Israeli nation. The Jews living here, who have made their state here, are but one sixth of the Jewish nation that is dispersed throughout the world, most or part of which is likewise today and will be tomorrow aspiring to return here. We never heard of an Arab Zionist movement, as a national movement of Arabs focused on this country.

Even most of those Arabs who call themselves refugees were not turned into refugees through any persecution on our part. They ran away of their own volition and turned themselves into refugees. And where are they living now? Within the territories of *Eretz Israel,* that territory whose geographic designation has for many years been *Palestine,* which includes both banks of the River Jordan. Moreover, an Arab who leaves that territory and moves to another Arab country does not move to foreign lands, but remains among his own people, his brethren, members of the same culture and language. He is not subjected to any foreign government but is living under Arab rule.

Let us assume however, for the sake of argument, that a Palestinian nation has already come into being, and is claiming its rights to this country. There still remains a cardinal question that all men of justice and conscience have to ask themselves. Let them take the map of the Jewish people, a map that unrolls both in time and in space to extend over the entire world. What has this nation given to the world

BEFORE ANY COURT OF JUSTICE

and what has it received from it? What has been its reward for all it has given? How has the world repaid its peaceful contributions over the ages, indeed in these very times, when the world's wickedness and ingratitude stand revealed more clearly than ever before?

After all that has been done to this nation within living memory in Europe, and what is continually being done to it in Eastern Europe, and what is about to be done to it in other parts of the world—what is it that it wants? It was at one time accused of shutting itself up in the ghetto and constituting a state within a state. It has given up any desire or claim to do so. It was accused of leaving the ghettoes and trying to permeate and subvert gentile society. It has given up any attempt to do so. It was accused of wanting to dominate other countries and nations. It has given up any ambitions in that direction—if it ever had any. It was accused of being the leader of all the various revolutionary movements in all the different countries. It has ceded that position, as well.

It has retreated on all fronts, withdrawn from all the causes for which it was persecuted and slaughtered. All it claims for itself is what all younger nations with much fewer rights and claims are granted or, as a matter of course, what is given to tribes and peoples who only yesterday emerged from the jungle or who only yesterday tried to throw the world back into the jungle by making total war on others.

It demands its own homeland—not just any homeland, but the land in which it became a nation, where it created those values that have become part of the civilised world, from which it was driven by force and which it is rebuilding and rehabilitating with its labour and sweat. It does not even ask the world to finance this unique enterprise, though the whole world is called upon to look after the upkeep of the Arab refugees. Nor does it ask anybody else to shed his blood for its sake. All it asks is once again to be allowed to return to this its land, and live and work here.

You are saying it is doing so at the expense of others. What others? Not at the expense of any other nation or state, because neither of these had been here before. And not at the expense of the Arabs living in this country, since the Jewish nation grants them all the civil rights of a minority freely reaping the benefits the Jews have brought to this country. The average living conditions of the Arabs in Israel are higher than in any other country, and the living standards of the Arabs in the "administered" areas has risen by over one quarter in the last three years.

But that does not satisfy them nor their righteous friends and supporters. They want another Arab state here, in addition to the 15 Arab states that already exist. At whose expense? The Jewish people, of course.

At the expense of the ancient, persecuted Jewish people for whom this is the only piece of land in the world which it is entitled to call its own home, the only place where it can say—here I am not a stranger.

Now, after the Six Day War, the territory of Israel extends over 90,000 square kilometres. As against this, the Arab nations have 11,000,000 square kilometres at their disposal—more than the whole of Europe. They have an entire continent, rich in natural resources which are only partly exploited, and numerous rivers which have not yet been harnessed and utilised.

Where then is that social justice that calls for a fair distribution of the world's wealth? Just try to make the calculation—11 million sq.km. for 100 million Arabs as against 90,000 sq.km. for 12 million potential Jewish citizens of the Jewish state. To simplify the calculation let us round off the figures;—not 11,000,000 sq.km. for the Arabs but only 10,000,000, and let us round off our own figures to our detriment; 10,000,000 Jews over 100,000 sq.km. You still arrive at a ratio of 10 persons per sq.km. for the Arabs and 100 persons per sq. km. for the Jews. In this cold calculation, history and sentiment, suffering and loyalty to the country have no part. It is an ultra-rationalist account, based strictly on the principles of equality and justice.

Do the Arabs then need a state? Or extra territories?

In the face of this simple calculation, can all those righteous upholders of justice and equality still dare to look us in the face? Is this not enough to shame all those mighty world powers for the wrong and evil they are trying to do us, the Jewish nation, from which they have already taken so much, whose blood they have already spilt so generously? How does it come about that almost everybody is weeping bitter tears for the suffering of the poor Palestinian Arabs who have the backing not only of 100 million of their own brethren, but also of 200 million Soviets and 800 million Chinese, not to mention India and Pakistan and half of France and the entire New Left in Europe and America?

Nor are these Arab nations poor; they are powerful oil states with tremendous territories and resources, and millions of inhabitants, members of their own nations, who are waiting in vain for the progress and development that is their due. Yet their sole desire, their sole ambition, their whole energy and zeal and cunning are focused upon this one little corner of the world that they call Palestine. Their enemy is not the poverty of their own people. It is not Christianity, as it once was. Nor is it the widespread practice of slavery in their own lands, or the Russian bear who is sinking his claws into them and will soon reduce them to the same state as Czechoslovakia. This tremendous Arab empire of fifteen states extending over what amounts to an entire continent has only one single enemy: the Jewish nation returning to its homeland and holding on to 90,000 square kilometres, most of it desert.

That is the enemy.

Look at the map.* And also do not forget to unroll the

---

*Inside front and back covers.

historic map of the past four thousand years, and in particular the Jewish map of the last thirty years.

These are the facts—the most shocking existential facts conceivable. (And we do not want to confuse the issue by dragging in the claims of eight hundred million Chinese to the almost empty continent of Asiatic Russia and Siberia. That is not our problem but may serve as a small reminder to the seekers of right and justice and equality.)

Had there in fact been such a court of justice in the world, we need not fear to bring our case before it, in full awareness of its truth and justice.

Yet there is no such court of justice. Why, then, did we bother with its imaginary proceedings?

For our own sakes, for the sake of those men of tortured conscience amongst ourselves and perhaps also for those men of goodwill in the rest of the world who may simply not have grasped the problem in its full dimensions—so that they may cast all guilt out of their hearts. No justice can be greater than ours, no undertaking more pure and holy. Let their conscience rest in peace. No evil whatsoever is being done here to the Arab nation. There can be no comparison between what they have and the small scraps left over for us. If those men of justice, those men of protest and dissent, of the old and of the new Left are indeed men of conscience and of goodwill to all, let them glance at this map of the Arab Empire and its tremendous wealth and the puny map of poor Israel—even in its present expanded boundaries. Will they still dare to look us straight in the eye and say that we are wrong and they, the Arabs, are right? Will they still dare to deny that if there is a national liberation movement in the world today which is truly fighting for a just cause, it is Zionism, the liberation movement of the Jewish nation?

Unless they be hypocrites. If they are Jews and refuse to admit this evident fact, then they are sick with self-hate.

(*Traitor* is too banal a word to be used in this context and does not go to the root of the matter.) If not, then they are tainted with Nazism, and carry that germ of irrational hatred for the Jews, the desire to put an end to the Jewish nation out of a guilt-laden conscience or simple envy.

There is still another possibility. Those who uphold the Palestinian Arab cause at our expense, may not be inveterate anti-Semites, nor be convinced that the non-establishment of still another Arab state is a historic evil, but may simply be following the progressive fashion, or consider the Arabs as their political allies in other matters; if they belong to the Right, because of Arab oil, or if they belong to the Left, because they find in them confederates in their denunciation of the U.S.A.

This is quite legitimate, in the world as it is. But let no one dress it up in terms of justice, equity and conscience. Let them be frankly cynical, like Hitler and like Stalin in the past and Brezhniev now. Only please, without any talk about lofty ideals and without crocodile tears for the poor Arab refugees!

12

JORDAN IS A RIVER NOT A STATE

As our examination has shown, the mother of the State of Israel was the everlasting yearning of the Jewish people for redemption from exile; and its father—the urgent need to save the Jewish people from physical and spiritual annihilation. And with all due respect to this father, it is a good thing that with us it is the mother who counts most.

By analogy, the mother of the so-called Hashemite Kingdom of Jordan was an abandoned, ownerless land, without people or heritage. Its father was an Imperialism that happened to cast its seed about at random, almost by an act of artificial insemination. It might be worth while pondering upon that fact, after it has failed to produce a nation or anything else whatsoever since its bastard birth. And in its present anarchical condition all that is left of it is the vestige of a half-Bedouin half-British-made king and a welter of Syrian, Iraqi and Pakistani troops with dozens of terrorist organizations, fishing in its murkiness for their multifarious and nefarious purposes.

There never was a state or a country by the name of Jordan, nor a people, nor a nation by that name. Jordan is the name of a river, a river whose size is totally disproportionate to its fame. Nevertheless it has certain ultra-individualistic tendencies and idiosyncrasies. There hardly is another river that coils and twists and circumambulates like the Jordan that follows a course almost as meandering and circuitous as that of the Jewish people. From the peaks of the Hermon down to the Dead Sea, the lowest spot on earth, the distance it has to cover is only 87 miles, but it makes this way in 155 miles, almost twice the actual stretch. Many are the adventures and obstacles it meets along its course. The swamps of the Huleh are muddy, but what does a little dirt matter to the chief river of the Holy Land! Then comes something more pleasant—the Lake of Kinneret, called after the Hebrew *Kinnor,* the soothing harp in whose shape it is moulded. The temptation to succumb to its charms and grow drowsy with pleasure is great, but the Keeper of Israel knows no sleep and neither does the River of Jordan. Reinforced by its brief respite it once again resumes its task, telling us, as it were, that even when everything is quiet on the surface, deep below the people of Israel never ceases to rumble as the Jordan waters never cease to flow. And then come the basalt rocks, the jungle and the desert that have to be traversed in order finally to end in that Sea which may be called Dead, but constitutes one of the richest mineral treasures on earth.

Yet it is not its physical singularity that has given our Jordan its historic renown, but all that has happened on its waters and shores, all the many natural and supernatural events that it has witnessed. For it has seen much in its long life: Many imperial armies have marched across it and along it. But the imprint they left was far less than that of Jacob, crossing it with his stick, that of Joshua, leading the people of Israel across it on dry land, and that of David who again re-crossed it on his way to the eastern bank—David whom others revere only because he has become holy to us and whose name would never have reached the corners of the earth unless we had revived his Kingdom here. Nor would the name of this country have spread far and wide had it not been for us and our connection with it.

There are politicians who think that pragmatism is the be all and end all, that one should heed neither history nor faith nor ideals. They speak about the Kingdom of Jordan as something substantial, a factor to be taken into account by them and the State of Israel. This approach might be right for every other place in the world, but it does not apply to this country.

Here there can be no pragmatism that goes against history. This would be as much of an impossibility as that the Jordan should flow back from the Dead Sea up to Mount Hermon. There is no power in the world that can turn the Jewish people back from its course. Nor can the Arab inhabitants on both banks of the Jordan be turned into a new "Jordanian" nation.

One can have no quarrel with the younger generation that was born to today's map and accepts the state of Jordan as an existing fact. They have no reason to doubt that there is some ethnic, national, historical and cultural reality behind this concept. After all, they hear about many new countries that are springing up in Africa these days, and though even about them the last word has probably not yet been spoken, they usually do stand for some tribal reality. In Jordan there is not even that. The entire state of Jordan is a product of accident and connivance.

In 1922 the river Jordan became the administrative boundary between the two parts of *Eretz Israel,* and the Jews' authority to build a national home was restricted to the West Bank. Subsequently Abdullah, by the grace of the British, was made king of the Bedouin tribes roaming that area.

But not only under the auspices of the British; indirectly he also ruled by the grace of the Jews. For in our eagerness to find "good" Arabs who would consent to the realisation of the Zionist ideal we sought out this Abdullah, a man who had no followers among the local Arabs and who would not have been there at all, and certainly not as a king, had it not been for the British. While Britain was our misplaced love, Abdullah and his kingdom were our misplaced hope. For the sake of this hope we neglected natural potential allies among the national and religious minorities—the Kurds, the Maronites and the Druze, who are all suffering from Arab oppression.

But in 1948, the first year of our statehood, if we had at least seen to it that this foreign dynasty on the other side of the Jordan should stay in Trans-Jordan! From the military point of view there was nothing to stop us from getting as far as the Jordan and dealing with Shechem (Nablus) and Hebron in the same way as we dealt with Lydda and Ramle. It was our unhappy love that betrayed us. And at a meeting in Jericho, of all places, we abandoned the entire central part of Cis-Jordan to Abdullah's rule.

Yet all to no purpose, for in the Western territories too, the Hashemites never managed to set up a nation, a culture or a state worthy of the name. There is no comparison between what we have accomplished in the past twenty years and what they have done.

Abdullah was assassinated, his son Tallal was declared insane, and so his grandson Hussein came to the throne. And again we believed that he was the one good Arab ruler, the one who would be our ally. What forlorn hopes! Dashed to the ground when in 1967 he opened fire, and issued orders to kill and destroy—women, children, old and young.

Now he is fighting for his throne and for his state, which can have no future because it has no past, which has no justification because it fills no need, not being a viable entity in any sense of the word. Saudia, Iraq and Syria all regard it as part of their own territories. Yasser Arafat's terrorists regard it as the bridgehead for the annihilation of Israel. And we?

We have the historic memory of the land of Reuben and Gad and half the tribe of Manasse, of the land of David and the Hasmoneans; we have a Divine promise and the temporal promise made by the fifty-two nations who ratified the Balfour Declaration according to which Trans-Jordan is part of the Jewish homeland; we have the recent memory of the lands bought there by the Zionist Organization right down to the thirties (the Rothschilds held lands in the Horan, Ussishkin bought lands in Moab). And in view of all this, are we once again going to sit on the fence, as passive observers of the events that may take place there?

We made two glaring mistakes in the Six Day War. We did not take Aqaba,* which could have been done with firing hardly a shot, so as to sever all contact between Jordan and Egypt and cut off all military supplies. This would have forced the Hashemite ruler either to negotiate for peace or to close shop. And then we failed to take the Gilead heights together with the Golan, so that the settlements in the Jordan Valley might be removed from the firing line.

Jordan was always a western protectorate, first British and then American. It was these western powers which always prevented us from doing what was called for. In 1956, during the Sinai campaign, our forces had already penetrated into the Hebron mountains and crossed the borders in Jerusalem, but a British ultimatum checked their advance. To this day the Western powers regard Jordan as a private possession which Israel must not touch. Yet Jordan is hardly sacrosanct. What happened in Libya is also likely to happen there, with the only difference that while Libya is far off, Jordan is as close as can be. When overnight the "good" Hussein went over to Nasser's camp and joined in the "good" fight for our annihilation, the West did not stand in his way.

Do we need much imagination to predict what will happen to us if the Iraqis, the Syrians, the Egyptians or Arafat's terrorists take over and line up against us along the Jordan?

It is our duty to intervene so that justice may be done to us and to others. The map of the Middle East must be revised through the emergence of natural national states. The artifact of Jordan is nearing its end. Even without any reference to historic rights and Biblical promises, Aqaba and Gilead are vital necessities. And in taking them no

---

*The Jordanian port next to Eilat.

violence will be done to any existing nation; the political sovereignty of these territories has already been infringed by our worst enemies. (If Canada were about to disintegrate and the Russians were going to take over, would the United States have a single moment's hesitation? Not likely. For this is no longer the same case as Vietnam.)

The Jordan as a borderline might be conceivable in the event of a real peace, with a real state, a civilised state. In the absence of such, the only true border can be the desert, a fact already recognized in ancient times when, like now, Trans-Jordan was the invasion route of savage nomadic tribes out to despoil the settled land. No state and no nation was ever founded there, not in Biblical times and not in our own era, and this was hardly happenstance.

The battle for the succession is brewing. And let it be remembered—the Jordan, as every decent encyclopaedia, Judaica and Britannica, will tell us, is the river that flows through the middle of Palestine, *Eretz Israel*.

The Hashemite Kingdom is merely the weakest link in the chain. Many other Arab states in the Middle East rest on equally ramshackle foundations. At the same time there are numerous minorities imbued with a deep ethnic and historic awareness and pride who yearn for independence, such as the Kurds and the Druze. They, too, have not yet spoken their last word. Nor can the boundaries of the various oil principalities which certainly represent neither nations nor states be regarded as final.

The map of the Middle East is still very much in a state of flux. Neither factually nor historically can the present borderlines be justified and perpetuated. The blatant hypocrisy of proclamations to the effect that territorial gains by force of arms are inadmissible—often heard at the U.N. from those powers who have the least right to make them —is self-evident. Until June 4, 1967 all territorial changes in the world—all achieved by force, of course—were not only legitimate but sacrosanct. But when Israel tried to defend herself and liberate the occupied areas of her own homeland, to establish safe boundaries where she might rest secure, then the change thus wrought suddenly became wrongful and illegitimate, and had to be reversed.

Any decent historian and politician will laugh out loud at such arbitrary statements. We are already witnessing numerous other territorial changes—and there will be many more—which are accomplished by main force, sometimes justly and sometimes not. The entire map of Africa is still shifting and changing, and in Asia, too, the lines are not yet firmly drawn, either between China and Russia or between India and China and India and Pakistan, or between Iraq and the Kurds and Iraq and Persia. Even in the centre and east of Europe the map is not final.

The least settled of all is the map of the Middle East. Most of the boundaries here were not drawn according to ethnic-historic criteria, through the impact of national liberation movements, but in the most artificial manner, to further imperialist interests or consolidate the rule of feudal dynasties. Everything here is still in the evolutionary and revolutionary stage, including the State of Israel which has already changed many a frontier and will yet help many an oppressed minority to attain its independence and in turn redraw the map. One of the major changes already brought about is the reversion of Egypt to her national boundaries through the Israeli presence on the Suez. The fact that Egypt has thus been shaken out of her pan-Arabist, or imperial Arabist, illusions is of immense significance not only for us but for the world at large, and not least for Egypt's own national development.

13

ISRAEL AND ISMAEL

1. This Is How It Started

THERE are no Arab refugees in the sense that the term "refugee" is normally used. Needless to say, no credence can be placed in the figures given by the Arabs. Anybody who is familiar with the Middle East and with Arab mentality, or who has merely followed their war bulletins, realises that the Arab sense of truth is somewhat flawed, or at least different from Western standards. This Arabian tale may be indicative: An Arab father wants to rest, and his children are making a noise. To quiet them he says, "In the market-place they are distributing olives free!" The children rush there. Ten minutes later the father quickly gets dressed, exclaiming, "What! In the market-place they are distributing free olives! Why am I sitting at home!"

In this way they make up similar stories and start to believe in them. So it is with regard to the refugees and with regard to their own strength. Fact and fiction are freely intermingled, not necessarily in order to prove a point but out of sheer indifference or playfulness.

In the case of the refugees, of course, the reasons are less innocent. Here it is a matter of political and financial gain. For over 20 years these so-called refugees have been living at the expense of others, least of all their Arab brethren but mainly other nations. Most of them prefer this parasitic existence to hard work. Those who work would not dream of having their names crossed off the charity lists, which of course include also those who have long since died or emigrated to Kuweit or elsewhere.

There has been many a war in the world. There also have been many, many refugees. So far, however, they have all been taken care of, primarily by their own people who looked after their daily wants and integrated them in their economy. That is how the Indians treated refugees from Pakistan, and the Pakistanis absorbed the refugees from India. That is how the Germans dealt with their refugees who were driven out of Poland and Czechoslovakia. Evidently, that is how the Jews handled their own refugees who were integrated and absorbed in Israel. International funds are used only for rendering first aid for the first year or two, after which the refugees or their host countries are left to fend for themselves.

Not so with the Arab refugees. No other nation in the world has ever shown such indifference to the fate of its own people. Theirs is a case of criminal negligence, which is not surprising to anyone who knows how Arabs treat each other during their frequent internecine dissensions. It is a kind of sadism unknown even by cannibals, who at least desist from eating members of their own tribe. During the numerous pogroms they inflicted on the Jews before the Jews had come to their senses and set up their own military forces that no longer relied on the protection of the British police, such horrors as the mutilation of live and dead bodies—cutting off their heads and sex organs, splitting open bellies and the like—were a common occurrence. In mitigation, however, it may be said that they practice no discrimination: They treat their own the same way. One of the prize examples is the political exploitation of their own refugees, whose actual suffering did not concern them in the slightest.

It is evident, therefore, that for the Arabs this is no humanitarian but solely a political problem. From the humanitarian point of view the problem could have been solved long ago. Of course Egypt could not have offered a solution, having to cater for her own population living in semi-starvation and disease, and which is far greater than the number of Palestinian refugees, even according to the fictitious and exaggerated figures cited by the Arabs. The other Arab states however, especially those which have recently been given an enormous impetus by the discovery of vast oil resources, could have easily done so. Israel in twenty years grew from a population of 700,000 to close to three million, taking in three times its original population. Most of the newcomers were poor, unskilled refugees. The oil-rich Arab states could easily have coped with half that number—according to their own bloated figures. They would thus have relieved the suffering of their own kinsmen and given a boost to their economies which are crying out for manpower.

In the wake of the Second World War and subsequent developments in other parts of the world, as many as 45 million people lost their homes and were classified as refugees. But only the Arab refugees were not re-absorbed by their own people. Moreover, of the 45 million refugees of the last 20 years only a tiny minority returned to their own country. For humanitarian reasons other solutions were preferable, and were duly found.

It should also be borne in mind that the Arab refugees were not driven from their lands, their villages and towns. They picked up their feet and fled. Those who stayed behind fared very well indeed. Apart from the right to organise gangs of saboteurs and go on the rampage, they enjoy all civil rights and their objective conditions in Israel are better than those of their fellow-Arabs living under Arab rule.

Those who left did so at the behest of their own over-zealous leadership despite the pleas of Israel's leaders to stay on. Once they had got them to leave, their leaders abandoned them to their own devices. They refused to take care of their wants, but merely used them as a political pawn in their war of annihilation against Israel. That this was their deliberate, stated purpose throughout these years is all too often ignored or intentionally forgotten. The total annihilation of the State of Israel was the declared objective not only of the Palestinian Arabs, but of the leaders of all the Arab states. Openly proclaimed in their horror propaganda and their schoolbooks, this objective has also figured prominently in the official planks of all Arab organizations and at all Arab conventions since Israel came into being. Nor was it, as some whose memory is poor or deliberately attenuated try to make out, a consequence of the refugee problem. On the contrary, the Arab objective—annihilation of Israel—was the cause of the refugee problem.

This is the fundamental point which can be concealed only from a generation that has never heard about the history of Zionism and the Arab struggle against it. It is only to such Western youngsters that the refugee problem can be presented as an outcome of Zionism and the foundation of the State of Israel, and not, as it really is, the outcome of Arab opposition to Zionism and the State of Israel.

We have already mentioned the pogroms the Arabs organised against the Jews from 1920 onwards, right after the Balfour Declaration, right at the beginning of organised Jewish settlement aimed at the establishment of a Jewish state in the country. When the state was finally set up in 1948, seven Arab states went to war against it; the indigenous Palestinian population, with few exceptions, remained idle onlookers or "sat on the fence." It was as a result of this war against a state established according to the resolution of the United Nations, and as a result of the wild incitement by the Arab leaders that the refugee problem arose. Right from the outset this contingent of artificially created refugees was designed for revanchist purposes. They were expressly told to leave in order that they might come back on the day of victory, to slaughter the Jews and take over their property. The whole story is highly reminiscent of the court scene where the accused is asked why he had killed his victim: "It all started this way, sir. He *returned* my blow and . . ."

It is essential that these facts be recalled also in order to correct another misrepresentation: the false comparison between the Arab refugees and the Jewish refugees in Europe.

2. When Analogy Becomes Demagogy

To refute the all too frequent analogy made by Jewish intellectuals in order to denigrate Zionism and Israel and thus give vent to their self-hate, or to flatter various pseudo-progressive and far from pseudo-hypocritical elements, no more than a minimum of intelligence, integrity and factual knowledge is required.

We may interject at this point that another equally fallacious analogy is often drawn between the modern horrors of Auschwitz and of Hiroshima. Again it is only the Western, free world that indulges in such analogies. In the progressive Communist world Auschwitz has been forgotten altogether, and only Hiroshima remains. What happened in Hiroshima? Hiroshima was a shocking event in view of the huge number of casualties caused by the first atomic bomb and their protracted suffering from the effects of nuclear radiation. The bombing of cities and civilian populations, however, was nothing new. The only innovation was that in ordinary bombings the casualties ran into thousands while here they reached hundreds of thousands. It still was no attempt at genocide, but only the use of a most cruel and radical weapon. No one can deny that it was used in the course of the war between the U.S.A. and Japan, nor will anyone venture to contend that if Japan—and above all Nazi Germany—had managed to develop an atom bomb before the Allies did, they would have used it without the slightest compunction. Mankind can in fact be congratulated on the fact that the U.S.A. won the race and not Japan or Germany. It may be legitimately argued that it might not have been necessary to use this weapon at a time when it was already evident that Japan would not be able to win the war. It is also a moot point whether, to spare the lives of so and so many tens of thousands of American soldiers who would have fallen if the war had gone on longer, it was permissible to use a bomb that had such fatal effects on a civilian target. However that may be, it is indisputable that the atom bomb was a means used by one combatant against another.

Does the same apply to Auschwitz? Was the extermination of six million Jews by means of poison gas the use of a cruel weapon by one combatant against another? Was the Jewish nation ever at war with the German nation? No. This was a case of deliberate, cold-blooded murder, of the killing of a nation that was neither a combatant nor an enemy in any political sense, for at that time it was a nation without a state.

Not that we are so proud of the distinction to have had six million of our people exterminated. It is a distinction we would gladly be without. On the other hand only those who ignore the singularity of this event, who ignore the fact that it was but the outcome and consequence of Jewish exile, can misapprehend what is going on in *Eretz Israel,* and disregard the singularity of our war of liberation.

Back to the other false analogy we started off with—the analogy between the position of the Jews in the various countries they live in, and the position of the Arabs in the State of Israel, either as citizens or as so-called refugees.

The Arab population within the boundaries of Israel-Palestine cannot be equated to the Jewish population anywhere in the world. This Arab population is in conflict with the State of Israel and with Zionism over the title to and possession of this country. Such was never the case with any Jewish minority in any country whatsoever. Even in pre-war Poland, where the Jews constituted a large minority of about 11 per cent, their struggle was for civil rights and economic status, but never for possession and rulership.

To go a step further: the Jews in the diaspora never had Jewish states surrounding or as neighbours to any non-Jewish state and threatening its existence. There was neither any danger of conquest from the outside nor of irredentist movements from the inside.

Last but not least—when the Jews in the diaspora, voluntarily or otherwise, left one gentile state they had to move by force of circumstances to another gentile state. As for the Arabs, when they leave of their own free will, or even should they be forced to leave the boundaries of the Jewish state—where do they end up? In exile, among some foreign nation? Far from it. They get to an Arab country, ruled over by fellow Arabs, where theirs is the official religion, theirs the predominant culture, theirs the official language, and where there are usually many members of their own families living as citizens of their own state.

Had the Arabs put their displaced persons problem solely on a humanitarian footing, it would have been solved long ago, and Israel would certainly not have been the last to lend a helping hand. But they themselves claim—and here they are quite right—that it is a strictly political problem. Hence there is no reason whatsoever why Israel should relate to it in any other way than as to a distinctly political problem, especially since to no small extent the State of Israel arose because of the political interpretation given to the human suffering of the Jews living as a minority. We therefore have a much more thorough understanding, and thus also a much more thorough solution of this problem than any outsiders, however sincerely they may be concerned.

We are in the best position to offer a satisfactory solution —because of our physical proximity and our familiarity with the people involved; because of our certain knowledge that eventually any solution proffered for their settlement in this country will be at the expense of our existence, our security and our independence; and because we as Zionists, and especially as revolutionary Zionists, have learned on our own blood and flesh what is the best political and most humanitarian solution to a problem of this kind.

3. Clash of Aspirations

The problem of the Arabs in *Eretz Israel* is not merely the problem of the so-called Arab refugees. That problem if it were really all, has much greater prospects of being solved under Jewish auspices, as long as the refugees are under our control, than when they are not under Jewish rule. For the Jews they are no political pawn. Under a Jewish government they can simply cease to be refugees and turn into citizens fully integrated in the life of the country. From the individual and humanitarian point of view there is nothing to prevent this from happening right away. Justly or unjustly, reasonably or unreasonably, however, the Arabs, or rather most of them, especially the younger generation and the intellectuals, are not satisfied with this kind of solution. Nor are they satisfied with such compromise offers as the establishment of a Palestinian state in part of Western *Eretz Israel*. They insist on the entire country, and there is some reason in this demand, assuming that there is a Palestinian nation. Anybody who makes this assumption can hardly agree to Jerusalem not being the capital of this Palestine, nor to Galilee, where there still is an Arab majority, being annexed to it. He will not forget that Ramle and Lydda and Jaffa and Acre were once inhabited by Arabs.

And here we say: precisely as Zionists we have the fullest understanding for this attitude. We acknowledge its valid conception of the indivisibility of this country. We respect the desire to live in a national state of one's own and to prefer a collective existence under difficult conditions in national independence to an easier individual life under foreign rule.

But comprehension does not imply consent, because such consent spells suicide for us. Any Palestinian state, not only in the whole of *Eretz Israel* but even in part of it, bears the seeds of ultimate destruction for the State of Israel. There is no room in so small an area for two states, each of them for historical and geopolitical reasons, not to mention emotional or demographic factors, naturally aspiring to possession of the other's territories.

Understanding for the subjective aspirations of our enemies—only their political aspirations but not their cannibalistic desires, their overt and covert wish to exterminate us—does not imply by any means that we also acknowledge the objective justice of their cause.

At this point it also seems worthwhile to make another distinction: that between Arab fighters crossing or trying to cross the border to attack Israeli military installations, to enter into battle with Israeli forces in the knowledge of potential death or capture, and outright murderers planting bombs in bus stations and cinemas or throwing hand grenades at civilian cars and killing women or children or men going about their ordinary business. In all our underground activities against the British we never attacked private British citizens, women or children. That famous Arab village, Deir Yassin, to which the Arab humanitarians keep harking back in their propaganda, was not a terrorist attack. It was a military action against a stronghold dominating the entrance to the then besieged city of Jerusalem, a stronghold which had given shelter to marauding gangs ambushing Jewish transport and civilians. In this assault there were also many fatal casualties on the side of the IZL and the FFI. In the house to house fighting that was necessary in order to take what was virtually a military camp, some 250 Arabs, including women and children who hid in their houses and refused to leave although asked to do so by loudspeaker at the beginning of the action, were killed. Killed in battle.

Fighters are not the same as killers. But even then, the

war waged by the first category, the real fighters, need not necessarily be a just war. What about the Nazis—were there no brave soldiers among them? Not all of them were Eichmanns or Mengeles, mere murderers of women and children. This alone, however, does not yet mean that Rommel was fighting a just war, even if he himself was no murderer but a true soldier. While all murderers are evil, not every evildoer is a murderer; which does not alter the fact that what he is doing may still be evil.

In the same way, the war the Arabs are waging against us is evil and unjust, whether it be waged by cowardly saboteurs choosing civilians for their target, or by the partisans of El Fatah or the armies of Sa'adat or the "chivalrous" legionnaires of Hussein.

There are some objective or pseudo-objective observers who contend that this is a conflict between two rights, two equally just causes. This we certainly deny. Granting, however, that it is so—have we Jews no right to be subjective? Why must we be objective in a war in which we are directly involved? Granted even that gentile Americans or Russians, the upholders of world justice, or the Indians who are so well-known for their integrity, or Frenchmen of De Gaulle's ilk are entitled to be objective. Why on earth should we, the Jews, be objective? After all, this is a question of our survival, our independence, our honour, our return to our homeland.

After all that has happened to us we are permitted to be selfish. Much greater and stronger nations are pursuing their selfish interests, though they can well afford to be altruistic and make concessions, as long as they are not made at the expense of their sovereignty and independence. These are the concessions the Arabs are asking of us. They are not willing to concede an inch of their territory, whether actually in their possession or, in their opinion, occupied by others.

We certainly cannot afford either such objectivity or such altruism. We cannot afford such generous concessions.

Throughout the years of the diaspora our generosity was greater than was warranted by our safety, and that is what led us to the brink of extinction. Our minds can only be as broad as our land, our patience cannot be stretched any further than its length. Our wish for appeasement cannot go beyond the limits of our own safety.

All this has been said on the assumption that we are really dealing with a conflict between equally just causes. In the light of true objectivity, however, this is not so. It is not true, as is sometimes contended, that Zionism ignored the Arab problem. The presence of Arabs in this country was never disregarded, and ever since the Balfour Declaration, Zionism has been acutely aware that the Arabs were opposed to it even in its minimum form. There were many who in their naiveté believed that by proving to the Arabs how much we were benefiting the country we might convince them and change their minds. In vain. Others were so naive as to think that by giving up the idea of an independent state we might be able to win them over. In vain. The truth is that in this respect the Arabs had a more straightforward understanding of the process of history than many a sophisticated Zionist. They realised that the Return to Zion was a serious matter, that it implied the return of the whole Jewish people to the whole of Zion. When moderate Zionists tried to persuade them that this was not what was meant, they looked upon them as frauds, as purveyors of a cheap ruse. Only abnegation of the idea of mass immigration, the essence of Zionism, would have pacified them and temporarily, of course, reconciled them to the existence of an autonomous Jewish minority.

Obviously, Zionism could not agree to this. Yet the presence of numerous Arabs in this country, including some with nationalistic aspirations, never deterred even the moderate Zionists from their goal. When Weizmann was asked in 1920 (there were less than 100,000 Jews in this country at the time), what about the Arab problem he, the extreme moderate, replied, "The choice is between a great injustice and a small injustice. If there is no Arab state in this country it will be a small injustice. If there will be no Jewish state, an *Eretz Israel* that is Jewish ('like England is English,' was the way he put it), the injustice will be great."

The truth of this definition became evident some twenty years later, when in submission to Arab opposition the Government of Great Britain and indirectly also all her western allies, not to mention the U.S.S.R., abandoned the Jews of Europe to their annihilation. What terrible calamity would have befallen the great Arab nation, had those six million Jews been saved in a Jewish *Eretz Israel?*

And from there we arrive at a most objective and just conclusion—if there is such a thing as justice in this world: Had those six million Jews indeed been rescued in this way, not only would it have been an act of justice towards the great Jewish nation which has contributed so richly to humanity and suffered so much for it, but it would have been a blessing for the whole of mankind. There is every reason to assume that such an operation would have impeded Hitler's swift rise to power, and would have proved a boon to the Middle East and indirectly also to the Arab states neighbouring the great Jewish state that would have arisen. The entire Middle East would have blossomed and its wealth would have been such that it would no longer have been so completely dependent on either the West or the East, but would have formed an effective buffer zone between the three continents.

Within this great state, on both banks of the Jordan as originally proposed and projected, and as dictated by the geopolitical situation, and with the river Jordan being utilised and serving as a link rather than a wasteful barrier, there would have been an Arab minority living in prosperity and equality.

Try to imagine what great achievements could thus have been attained, had it not been for the wickedness and foolishness of the gentiles. And compare this with the projected achievements of a Palestinian or Hashemite state, another state of the type of Syria or Iraq. Is that all the Arabs need for their happiness? Have they already done everything they could and should have done for the sake of their own people?

Owing to the wickedness of the gentiles—the British who derived little satisfaction from their own perfidy, and the Arabs with their vast lands and numerous states—Israel's salvation could not be accomplished amicably and peacefully before the extermination. An ocean of blood had to be crossed in Europe and a river of blood traversed in this country before the much smaller vision could be realised, in a constant tug-of-war with the Arabs.

Such terms as *evil* and *wicked* may not be common usage in discussing political problems which are normally treated as a matter of interests, beyond good and bad. Yet there are countless contemporary examples of pure evil in the field of politics; actions that have no rational legitimation and that cannot be explained on the grounds of interests alone. Biafra, Auschwitz, the Leningrad trials, the imprisonment of Jews because they want to leave the land of socialist "freedom"—all these cannot be attributed only to a cool calculation of political interests; they are manifestations of intrinsic evil.

To counter the obstacles put in our way we have one more decisive asset in our favour. This is the fact that it is the wish of the Jewish people to be saved in and through this land—for all eternity. Since the *justice* of its cause alone has proved insufficient, it is reinforced by the *strength* this cause generates.

It is against the background of this reality that we should view the problem of the Arabs in *Eretz Israel,* to arrive at the best and most realistic solution, which it is our duty not only to perceive ourselves but also to proclaim openly for others.

4. Solution of the Arab Minority Problem

Had it not been for British encouragement, Nazi assistance, past and present Soviet Communist support, coupled with the personal and dynastic ambitions of various Arab families, the collective opposition of the Arabs to Zionism would never have taken the course it did.

Zionism no doubt also did and does receive support from anti-Semitism and the political interests of various world powers, but here external factors are used in the furtherance of an original, independent goal, rooted deep in the consciousness of millennia. The Arab national movement here, however, is totally new, a creature that would never have come into being or grown as it did without this outside assistance.

The outcome of the struggle so far also has some significance. After all, what did we set out with? We had neither strength nor numbers on our side. That we got as far as we did against an organised, deliberately aroused majority, and in spite of British perfidy, is by itself evidence not only of our stronger physical prowess but also of our greater will-power.

Just as most of the world is unaware of the fact that a vast portion of the Arab population in this country has not been living here for centuries but came here in the last few decades in the wake of local prosperity—and not for religious or patriotic reasons—it is also unaware how footloose this population is. They do not realise how easy it was for them to leave during the war, nor do they realise that from 1948 to 1967, when Samaria and Judea* were under Arab rule, as many as 370,000 Arabs emigrated from there to Kuwait or overseas.

---

*Currently referred to as "the West Bank."

This does not mean that the frustration of defeat, coupled with incitement from outside, strong ambitions for leadership and a real attachment to the country on the part of a few, may not be enough to feed a national movement, especially when so much is being done by all and sundry to help it along.

The past, as we have shown, has proved that all Zionist attempts to win the Arabs over to their side and reconcile them to the idea of full Jewish national independence, have failed. Since the Jewish nation has no other option if it wants to live as a nation—and it has proven its desire to survive as such for two thousand years, by emerging intact both from the Christian and the Nazi holocausts, and recently also from the Soviet stranglehold—and since for the Arabs it is not a question of life and death as they have fifteen alternative states of their own, there can be no doubt that we must continue our own liberation movement in full awareness of the justice and inevitability of our cause and in full consciousness of our own strength. Like the watchword of the sounder elements among the Jews of the diaspora, *Never Again,* our watchword here must be: *WE ARE HERE TO STAY.* This is what the Arabs must be told.

They have three alternatives open to them, and no other:

One is the course they are adopting now: belligerence. They have been following this warlike course for decades, first by means of marauding gangs, then by means of massed armies, running the entire gamut from knives and axes to missiles and Migs. We have won three major rounds and with each expanded our territories, liberating additional parts of our homeland contrary to our own conscious designs. We shall win the next round too, should it be forced upon us, which will lead to the final consolidation of all the areas liberated in the Six Day War, however willing (and foolish) we might have been to retreat from some of those territories now. The boundaries will once again be extended to areas like the Gilead, that are vital to our security, and of no little historical and economic importance. The losses will no doubt be greater than they have been up till now, but still less than any concessions might cost us. For the Arabs are firm in their original resolve: the extermination of Israel.

Those who hold out the threat of Russian intervention can hardly frighten us. It is highly likely that this threat is merely another Soviet blackmail attempt. The Soviets have already made similar blusters in Persia, in Greece, in Cuba and in Berlin, backing down as soon as they found out that extortion did not work. As for the Russians who are already here, Israel can beat them also, and they know it only too well. That is why they are putting a curb on the Arabs, trying to obtain for their vassals and themselves a re-opened Suez Canal, the Sinai and new military bases, by amicable means through Gunnar Jaring and perhaps with the assistance of some American Chamberlain making another trip to a Middle Eastern Munich. The despatch of massive forces from Soviet Russia to this front is a much more difficult matter. This is not Czechoslovakia which has a land border with Russia; nor even Finland. Tremendous logistic difficulties combine with the risk of another world war. Anyone who may think that this could be a means of extortion and intimidation, that the threat of another world war will cause the Western countries to compel Israel to submit, is quite mistaken. Not only are we not Czechoslovakia of 1968 where the Russians could simply march in with all their massive strength; we also do not happen to be Czechoslovakia of 1938 which submitted to the pressure of a scared and witless Western Europe.

Then it was Poland, a much weaker country than Czechoslovakia, which by the resistance it put up to Hitler caused the outbreak of the Second World War. Is there anybody today who dares blame her? Did she not save the world by so doing? Had Czechoslovakia started the war one year earlier, in 1938, she would no doubt have saved the world many millions of lives and rid it of an evil incubus so much the sooner.

The blackmail of another world war is not likely to deter the State of Israel. Undoubtedly it will be a catastrophe for the world at large but first of all it will be a catastrophe for us. But we have made up our minds that *we are here to stay*.

This the world should know and remember. But above all, it is something the Arabs must be told for their own good. If they continue along the course they have adopted, if war is what they prefer, they will continue to lose and we will continue to expand and consolidate. For we have no option. All we have to fall back on is our own strength and resolution. Again, the Arab residents of this country stand little to profit from a war like that. Hundreds of thousands who are now living here peacefully will again be doomed to the life of refugees, to being cooped up in refugee camps, to the loss and destruction of their property.

But they do have another alternative, particularly the Arab inhabitants of this country: They have the alternative of peace and reconciliation.

They have the alternative of reconciling themselves to the existence of the State of Israel, as a fact, however just or unjust. They can accept their fate, which should not be too difficult for Moslems brought up on the deterministic, fatalistic creed *"kullu min Allah,"* everything comes from God. Allah has proved that he wants this country to come back into the hands of the sons of Abraham, Isaac and Jacob. Neither Allah nor Muhammad ever promised this land to the sons of Ismael. They have enough of their own. And if submission to the divine will and the commandments of the Koran fails to enforce this acceptance, the facts of Jewish mass settlement, of Jewish industry, of the Israeli Army should have the necessary persuasive power. They all clearly spell out one thing: This is the Land of Israel.

The better alternative, therefore, is to become reconciled

to the facts as they are. This is what a quarter of a million Arabs living in the State of Israel before the Six Day War did. Individually they were better off than ever before and many, if not all, had reconciled themselves to being an Arab minority in a Jewish State for all eternity. This is the second option open to those million Arabs now living within the territories of the greater State of Israel.

Even now, while hostilities are still going on, the State of Israel is proceeding in these new territories as though there had never been any occupation or animosity. As long as there are no overt acts of terror, life there is not only calm and peaceful but even prosperous. There is no other instance in history where under conditions of such conflict and hostility between nations and countries such a policy of "open gates" should be followed, where thousands of students are free to travel to the Arab states to study—where friendliness to Israel is hardly part of the curriculum—and then come back here. Under such conditions it is unheard of, hitherto, that there should be free trade relations with countries that impose a strict boycott against Jews and any dealings with them; yet a considerable portion of the Arab intellectuals and former civil servants, who remained behind in Israel, go on receiving money from Hussein, the aggressor in the Six Day War who refuses to make peace, and pays these men so that they should not collaborate with Israel. Tens of thousands of refugees under Jewish rule are finally becoming productive, earning their own living and no longer feeding like parasites on others.

There are no bounds to Jewish-Israeli generosity once the local Arabs reconcile themselves to living as a minority in the State of Israel.

But nevertheless, whoever advocates a nationalist Jewish policy that knows no compromise on the question of national sovereignty and independence and puts national above individual interests must, more than anyone else, respect the attitude of those Arabs who refuse to accept the bribe of full equality in exchange for reconciliation and appeasement. Our Jewish character and our own self-interest induce us to accord full equality to the Arab minority in the State of Israel, not as a bribe but as a simple duty we owe to ourselves and our regime. Yet far be it from us to deny the Arabs the right to look upon such civil equality as a mere substitute for their aspirations to political independence. Precisely as Zionists we must respect the wishes of a minority not to live as a minority in a state where another nation constitutes the majority. This is the very thing we are constantly telling the Jewish people living as minorities in so many countries—including those where they enjoy equal rights, not only formally, but even actually: do not go on living under foreign rule.

For this reason we can but openly say to the national-minded Arabs: we fully respect your desire to live in an Arab state. But not here. This is *Eretz Israel* and will remain so forever. This is not the sole country you have. Anyone who wants to live under Arab rule deserves our fullest respect and even more: *our active help to emigrate and build up his life in such a state, outside Palestine, the Land of Israel.*

In fact this is the solution which appears to proffer not only the least evil, but the greatest possible good. It is best for us and for them. It serves the interests of peace in the Middle East and leads to economic progress. It is conducive to a truly fraternal relationship. Segregation is essential for the sake of peace; not segregation in the individual and derogatory sense that means discrimination. Any Arab wishing to stay in the State of Israel may choose whether his children should attend mixed or segregated schools. What is meant here is political segregation, not by the partition of the country which has proved impossible in all respects, but through the voluntary emigration of those Arabs who prefer a political life of their own.

This solution for minority problems has proved its

efficacy particularly in our times. In the long run it is also the most humanitarian. After much bloodshed, the dispute between Turkey and Greece was finally solved in this way, by a major population exchange after the Great War. Except in Cyprus there are accordingly no longer any territorial disputes between these two countries. As a result of the Second World War some 12 million Germans fled or were evicted from Poland, Czechoslovakia and what was formerly East Prussia, to Western Germany. This was considered a perfectly justified move since Germany was the aggressor country trying to invade and swallow up her smaller neighbours. Although the Germans had been living in the provinces of Silesia and the Sudetenland for close on 800 years and had been responsible for their development and prosperity, the Poles and the Czechs invoked their eight-hundred-year-old historic claims to these territories. The Communist leaders of these states, in making this population transfer, did so not only in order to secure their borders or to punish the German imperialists, but also in the name of a national return to the land of their forefathers. But no such historic reasons were available for East Prussia, which was annexed by Soviet Russia, the name of the capital Koenigsberg being converted to Kaliningrad. It was enough for the Russians to have won the war and to be firmly resolved to expand their boundaries and remove all Germans from the annexed territories.

At the very time this is being written a further step in the reconciliation between West Germany and Poland is taking place. Germany having recognized the Oder-Neisse line as the western border of Poland, it has been decided to enable the million or so Germans still left in Poland to leave and cross over to West Germany, despite the fact that they had been living in West Poland for hundreds of years and were deeply ensconced there, as in their own homeland.

Such population exchanges were not confined to Germany, the country that was vanquished in the Second

World War. Between the U.S.S.R. and Poland, too, millions of inhabitants were exchanged. From enormous territories in Eastern Poland which were annexed by Russia, some 2.5 million Poles were shifted westwards in exchange for 1.5 million Ukrainians and Byelorussians who were transferred to the East. This was done in an officially organized operation, and undoubtedly the population being transferred was not consulted. It was assumed as a matter of course, and with no little measure of justice, that these people would prefer to live in their own country rather than as a minority in another country, although both enjoyed a communist regime.

Then again, during the fifties hostilities broke out between India and Pakistan, two respected members of the U.N. Both of them are extremely active on behalf of a just peace in the Middle East—that is, another Arab state on top of the 15 there already are, and the *de jure* liquidation of Israel (according to Pakistan) or her *de facto* liquidation (according to the more moderate view of India). Both India and Pakistan insist on the million Arab refugees being returned to the whittled down territories of the State of Israel. Yet both these peace-loving nations have furnished us an excellent example, not by the bloody wars they have conducted, but by the solution they have found for their minority problem. As many as 15 million Indians and Pakistanis were transferred, and not in any orderly, humane fashion. About a million died on the way, entire regions changed their demographic structure, millions were torn from the land they had been living on since time immemorial. Not all problems between India and Pakistan were thus resolved. The problem of Kashmir—a kind of large, isolated Gaza Strip—still exists. But there can be no doubt that most of the tension has been allayed.

All these transfers and exchanges involving millions of people, were carried out in recent times, as the modern solution for tension-provoking demographic and national problems. There is no cogent reason why the same course should not be adopted with respect to the Arab minority in *Eretz Israel*.

Its roots in this country are certainly more tenuous than were those of the Germans in Silesia and Sudentenland, and of the Poles in former East Poland or of the Pakistanis in northern India.

We, in fact, have already performed our part of the exchange deal by taking in a million Jews from the Arab countries, including the Jews of Iraq and Lybia who had been living there close to two thousand years, longer than the Arabs who got there only with the expansion of Islam.

As Zionists, moreover, we have adopted this course of millions of Jews leaving the diaspora. We ourselves regard it as the best possible solution for a minority living under foreign rule, even where that minority is tolerated. There were Jewish communities in Europe which had been living in the same countries for over a thousand years before they left to return to their ancient homeland, and—a no less important aspect—to live under an independent, Jewish government. As Zionists we tell even the Jews of the United States of America, where despite the activities of a few anti-Semitic groups and certain disquieting sociological developments, they appear to be living under the best conditions: Get up and leave, go home, back to Zion, your two-thousand-year-old homeland, because it is better for people to live in their own country, not only to be rid of oppression but also to be no longer dependent on the *good graces* of a majority: Prepare to volunteer—better than being forced.

It is not our business here to refute Arab and Soviet propaganda about the living conditions of the Arabs in *Eretz Israel*. We might, however, point out that the Jews of the U.S.S.R. have good reason to envy the Arabs living in *Eretz Israel*. The Soviet Jew would gladly change places with the "oppressed" Arab who lives under Israeli rule.

The Russians claim we oppress the Arabs. We in turn

bemoan the Russian treatment of our brothers in the Soviet Union. But there is a solution to this tug-of-war—simple, intelligent, gentle; in short, an "intelligentle" solution.

I am not going to suggest an exchange. The deal would not be quite fair because there are three million Jews in Russia and we have only one and a quarter million Arabs —though we could probably provide another million. Besides, the Russian deal with Poland was not all that fair, either; after World War II Russia took in only about one and a half million Ukrainians and Byelorussians for the two and a half million Poles shifted to Poland. Population transfers are something the Russians know quite a lot about, and we have a great deal to learn from them. But suggesting an exchange would not be realistic. Though the Russians love the Arabs dearly and admire their many talents, their love does not extend so far as that.

What we do suggest is that Russian Jews be granted the same conditions in the U.S.S.R. that the Arabs are enjoying in Israel. And I do not mean only the Arabs who were living in the States of Israel before the Six Day War, who were full citizens with equal rights, but also Arabs living in the new territories which the Russians and others claim have been occupied.

It would be fit and proper if the Russian Jews enjoyed the same conditions we offer to our oppressed Arabs. No more. And no less.

It would be fit and proper if the Russian Jews enjoyed the same suppression of freedom of speech we practice with our oppressed Arabs; if they were allowed to set up their own Yiddish or Hebrew Schools, just as the Arabs of Israel have their own schools; if Jewish university students were allowed to travel from Moscow and Odessa to Jerusalem—like the Arab students, given free transportation and safe conduct to and from Nablus, Gaza and Hebron to Cairo or Beirut.

It would be helpful if Russian Jews could establish a

Zionist party in the U.S.S.R.—like the pro-Russian, pro-Sa'adat Communist Party flourishing here—not, heaven forbid, to support enemies of the regime, but simply to express their love for Israel.

It would be no more than ethical if the Jews languishing in Russian prisons were given the same privileges that Israel offers to Arab criminals—such as legal counsel appointed for their defence and visits from their families and the Red Cross.

And it would be only human to accord the Russian Jews a fundamental human right—THE RIGHT TO LEAVE.

This elementary right we grant freely to all those Arabs who want to live in a state of their own. We not only advise them to go ahead and do so, but are willing to organize the exodus—a relief not only for us but also for them.

For in all truth, there are good reasons why they should be frustrated, especially the younger generation and the intellectuals who have been aroused to Arab nationalist activity but have missed the boat. By the time they woke up, Jewish revival was forging ahead proudly. All their attempts to initiate colonial liberation movements have failed because the principles on which these movements are based have no relevance. There can be no Mau Mau here and no FLN, as the Jews in Israel resemble neither the British in Kenya nor the French in Algeria. The Arab pretence that they constitute such a movement—they are trying to make the rest of the world believe it—cannot be sustained for any length of time because its patent untruth is bound to become evident. The Jewish rulers here are neither colonialists nor imperialists trying to expand their homeland at the expense of another nation in order to exploit it, and the Arabs here are not a nation exiled from its country and deprived of its independence.

Nevertheless, the psychological frustration is there, as well as a goodly dose of hatred and antagonism.

The youth and the intellectual strata of such a majority

cannot simply turn into a loyal minority, accepting a new reality. Many Arabs who would secretly like to make their peace with this reality do not dare to do so for fear of appearing to betray their cause. Obviously, any state and government must require all its residents to report and counteract subversive elements. The Arabs are not in an enviable position. They are between the hammer and the anvil. The Israeli anvil is physically the stronger, and more tempting from the material aspect. It can offer a far higher standard of living and a much greater measure of individual freedom than any of the Arab states. But there also is the hammer of the underground organisations that threaten to continue the war, and of the secret national longings of the individual Arabs.

It is only fair to try and understand this unfortunate position. Once it has been fully understood, there can be no escape from a frank and open approach. As Zionists who expect the Jews in the diaspora, however comfortable their life there may be, to leave and re-unite in their own country, we can but advise the Arabs to do likewise—to pick one of the numerous Arab states in order to live a full Arab life there. Any further attempt at violence through external war or internal subversion is only likely to culminate in their own mental and physical suffering.

No useful purpose can be served by discussing the solution of the refugee problem in terms of fanciful, destructive visions that attempt to reverse the wheels of history by bringing hundreds of thousands back to this country. (And if to Shechem [Nablus], why not to Acre and to Jaffa and to Ramle and to Lydda which were abandoned 20 years ago!) This solution can bring neither acceptance nor peace but only a continuation of the conflict. The advocates of such idle schemes would do much better to support a solution similar to that they themselves have used to such good effect. Turkey, Russia, Poland, Germany, India, Pakistan have carried out population transfers involving tens of millions. Can they not see that this course also offers the best basis for lasting peace here?

Even now there is a constant clandestine emigration of Arabs. Just as political revolutionary Zionism, as preached by Herzl, rejected gradual immigration in favour of organized evacuation with the aid of all available national and international resources, the idea of a similar organised evacuation of those Arabs who do not wish to live as a minority in an *Eretz Israel* ruled by Jews, should be openly put on the agenda. The funds and the organisational resources are bound to be forthcoming. And the developing oil countries, from Kuweit to Libya, are crying out for manpower.

Presumably most of the peasants, the *fellaheen*, will prefer to stay where they are and go on cultivating their lands; no one will interfere with them. Already they are benefiting from the improved agricultural techniques introduced by the Israelis at a pace inconceivable under any Arab regime. From primitive agriculture and artisanship they are fast advancing into the modern era. The urban youth and the intellectuals, however, are driven to subversion and sabotage by the very fact that there is no peace and that to their minds Israel's withdrawal or liquidation are attainable goals. This evidently cannot be permitted. Nor is it likely that they would wish to live permanently under Jewish rule. They are the candidates for the suggested move to one of the Arab states. There is no reason whatsoever why under a Jewish government the mass emigration to developing Arab states or to Canada, Australia, Latin America which has been going on for the last twenty years, should come to a halt.

Zionism is fully entitled to proffer this solution. A movement that exhorts its own people to leave countries they have been living in for centuries to return to their ancient homeland which they left 2,000 years ago, certainly has the right to offer a similar solution to the Arabs—who never regarded *Eretz Israel* as their ancient homeland, who never achieved statehood in this country, and for whom, moreover, it is not the only place where they can attain statehood, as it is for us. Political Zionism presented to the Jews the idea of an open, planned exodus, with international consent and assistance. Many Jews objected to this course, sought alternative solutions and found it hard to detach themselves from the countries they were living in. The Arabs need neither a Balfour Declaration nor an international mandate nor a conquering army. They can simply go to their own countries to live among their own brethren. Thus, of the three alternatives—the only three—open to the Arabs, this is the most modern, effective and humanitarian solution.

To sum up: Anyone who wants to stay here under a Jewish government is welcome to stay and will have all civil rights extended to him. Anyone who wishes to carry on the war is free to try his hand. He will be beaten as those before him were beaten over the last fifty years, and only help to strengthen the position of the Jews in this country. Those who wish to live in an Arab state and not under a Jewish regime are free to leave. This, under the right conditions, also offers the ideal solution for the major part of the Arab minority that has been living in the State of Israel since 1948.

14

THREE POINTS OF NO RETURN AND THREE STAGES OF SALVATION

WHEN the first Israeli paratroopers managed to fight their way to the Western Wall, a tremor of excitement passed through the entire nation. The tremor was felt no less by the modern, non-observant Jews of the U.S.A. and the U.S.S.R. than by the orthodox residents of Meah She'arim with their phylacteries and prayer shawls. Every soldier in his armoured car, in the far reaches of the Sinai, felt it passing through his flesh.

Why this extraordinary emotion? If the Western Wall is a religious symbol, evidently our religion must be of a singular variety. Similarly, if it is a national symbol, then our nationality is of a singular kind.

Formerly the Western Wall was referred to as the Wailing Wall. We would come there to mourn the loss of our past greatness and independence. When in the fourth century Jerusalem passed into the hands of the Christians, the Byzantine soldiers would receive a bribe to allow the Jews, once a year, to weep an extra hour at the ancient Temple Wall. They had the double satisfaction of the money they received and of seeing Jews prostrate themselves in tears.

The Wall continues to be revered in remembrance of the Temple that stood on the hill behind it, but it no longer is a wailing wall, despite the fact that no Temple is there yet.

The liberation of the Western Wall, beyond revealing once again the deep significance it holds for every Jew, also brought to light another fact of which until then only a few had been aware. The archaeologists who began digging there showed that the Wall goes much deeper down than might have been conjectured from that part which was visible hitherto. It is two and a half times as deep—or as high—a truly monumental structure. It also portrayed that, like the Western Wall, the Jewish people is much deeper, taller and mightier than it appeared to be at first sight. Many layers of the nation, resembling those buried rows of stone beneath the visible part of the Wall, were touched by a thrill of joy and identification that laid bare the depths of its solidarity.

The Wall has not yet been uncovered to its full extent. And future historians may well wonder which was the greater achievement of the Six Day War: the physical liberation of major parts of *Eretz Israel* or the psychological liberation of the Jewish nation.

Five years ago, when I had been saying that the Jews of California are like the Jordan Valley, the Jews of Boston like Jericho, the Jews of Leningrad like Shechem and Hebron, I was still denounced as a mystic. Now the truth of this statement is becoming more and more evident. The solidarity and oneness of the Jewish nation is far deeper than might have been thought.

Like the nation, so the land. For long periods both have been torn and divided, whole sections overlaid with foreign débris, half-forgotten and forsaken. But at a time of grave dangers and challenges, in the hour of greatness, the divisions heal and buried treasures are uncovered. Springs are found in the desert. Sparks of Jewishness are suddenly kindled in seemingly dead embers of the nation.

And that is another reason why no withdrawal from any of the territories recovered can be sanctioned. On the face of it this might seem to be a mystical, romantic, irrational, almost surrealistic reason. But in view of all that has happened to the Jewish people in the last thirty years, in the War of Liberation and the Six Day War, and in view of what is going on in the U.S.S.R. at present, it might be just as well for the hard-boiled rationalists and realists to revise their concepts, at any rate as far as the Jewish people is concerned.

Those parts of *Eretz Israel* that have been liberated with the nation's blood and love cannot be given up. They are the Jewish people's ancient homeland. There is no political precedent for such a move. Our right to these areas is much greater than the Russian title to what was formerly known as East Prussia or Poland's right to claim the Oder-Neisse line as her border. The Jordan and the Suez are our Oder-Neisse line. West Germany was willing to cede her claim to the territories lost in World War II. It is only fitting that the Arabs should give up their claim to the territories they lost in a war they launched by closing the Straits of Tiran, moving up their entire armour through the Sinai against the Israeli border, opening fire from the Old City walls on the peaceful Jewish residents of Jerusalem, and inflicting constant death upon the farmers of the Huleh Valley and the Tiberias region.

The present boundaries are the main safeguard for Israel's security. They also are the best and only guarantee for the country's economic independence and development. They are what make us into a geopolitical factor, whose alliance—and neutrality—is worth having. They protect us from being once again protected Jews—like the Schutzjuden of the Middle Ages, dependent on the good graces of the gentiles.

Also from the point of view of our own sense of history and self-esteem such a withdrawal is inconceivable. It goes against our inherent patriotism, our firm conviction that we are not engaged in a campaign of conquest and colonisation, but are coming back to Zion, our home. Home, *habaita,* is the watchword of the Jews of Soviet Russia. The cession of Shechem (Nablus) and Hebron and Jericho would mean that we have no claim to Tel-Aviv and Haifa, either. Our own sense of justice and right which gives us the strength to enforce our claims is bound to crumble. Not only is there no power in the world that has the right to demand that we give up our natural, historical claims and aspirations, but neither are we, who are already living in this country, entitled to make such a decision. This is the homeland of the entire Jewish people—the land of our forefathers and our descendants, that belongs to us as well as to the millions of Jews in Russia and in America. Some have already taken possession; others have done so, though in absentia. And others must have the right reserved to them, for tomorrow.

Withdrawal for the sake of peace is a dangerous chimera. No true, lasting peace can be bought in this way. Such concessions will merely feed the Arab lust for war. Once we are again with our backs to the sea, they will think it so much the easier to throw us right in—and have done with it.

Beyond that, however, it is a betrayal of our own past, and of the future of those millions who are still in the diaspora. For the sake of an immediate selfish urge for a short-lived breathing space, a moment's peace, we shall be imposing on the coming generation the obligation to wage another war to regain the same territories we are holding today. If, as in all likelihood will be the case, especially in the Sinai, the U.S.S.R. invades the evacuated areas in full force, at the invitation of her "socialist friends," the very existence of the State of Israel will be in jeopardy. Then we might indeed be wiped out before any Western power, should it be so inclined, can come to our aid. What Russian occupation of the entire Middle East would mean to the security and peace of the world need hardly be spelt out in detail. But it could happen only too easily. Israel's present borders are the only effective safeguard against such an eventuality, because it is only within these borders—four times as short as the pre-1967 armistic lines while providing a far deeper strategic space—that Israel can stop the Red deluge.

Such a retreat would also imply a counter-revolution, undoing the revolution that the Jewish people throughout the world has been undergoing in recent years; a people re-inspired with a love for this country and a sense of solidarity with the State of Israel which it has come to regard as its homeland. Israel, for the Jewish people, is no longer a refuge for the persecuted, but has become a new challenge for its tremendous creative potential.

For that Western Wall not only burrows deep underground, but also rises up high, as a symbol of the lofty aspirations embodied by the Temple that once stood on the hill behind it.

There are, indeed, Jews who keep asking: Is this really all? Does not the Jewish people have a spiritual destiny, as well? Does the purely physical survival of the nation warrant all these efforts?

Frequently these questions are posed in self-justification in order to be absolved of the need to come here, though the same Jews who pose them pray for the Return to Zion three times a day. Having been deprived of the excuse that the land is barred to them, they have found a new subterfuge: Maybe it is a land inhabited by Jews, but where is their Judaism?

But there are also those who in all innocence and without hypocrisy are concerned about the idealistic, Jewish aspect, our inherent moral pathos that aspires to higher values than the mere solution of physical problems.

It is pointless to try to convince the hypocrites. Suffice it to say that it is no more difficult to be an observant Jew following the Jewish commandments in *Eretz Israel* than in the diaspora, and that the dangers of assimilation and mixed marriage are certainly smaller. Let all those who are truly concerned about Judaism first come here, where if they wish they can try to modify attitudes according to their own lights in line with democratic practice, as citizens of the State. Above all they should be reminded that living in *Eretz Israel* is a primary, fundamental commandment of the Jewish religion. When the land is no longer lying waste under foreign rule, living in the diaspora is a cardinal sin.

To those who are seriously worried about the Jewish aspect of the State of Israel it is essential to bring home a basic theological point relating to the process of salvation and the sequence in which it can and ought to be accomplished. There is no denying that political Zionism which brought about the establishment of the State and the liberation of the country was mainly a movement of Jews who were not necessarily inspired by religious motives and frequently did not stem from religious circles. The reasons for this have already been outlined. Yet any religious Jew must ask himself: Why was this task assigned to the non-observant Jews?

The Talmudic sages have given the answer in their usual concise fashion: "Yiftah in his generation is like Samuel in his." Yiftah's social background was dubious. The son of a prostitute, he was an obscure company commander on the East bank of the Jordan. But when an enemy threatened to attack the tribes of Israel he was summoned to conduct the war against him; upon his victory, he was made a Judge, a leader of the people. Samson was another who did not distinguish himself by his religious observance and moral life. But again he saved the people of Israel from their enemies, and of him, too, the Jewish sages said that he was like Samuel the Prophet in his generation.

Our sages were perspicacious enough to realise that at the time of the Judges the task of the nation was to liberate and settle the country and overcome all external enemies. Those who performed this function were no less great than the prophets of another generation whose task it was to raise the people to a higher spiritual-moral level. Similarly we are entitled to look upon our own generation as one which has been assigned the task of saving the body of the nation, its physical existence, and of liberating and rebuilding the land in its material aspect, in the assurance that spiritual revival will follow.

That this should be the sequence in which salvation is accomplished is also confirmed by Ezekiel's famous prophecy of the dry bones (Chap. 37). The valley was filled with dry bones—dry in the physical or perhaps also in the spiritual sense. They moved up closer to each other "and sinews and flesh came upon them, and the skin covered them over." To wit, first it was the body of the people that came to life. It was only then, when physical existence had been restored, that the Prophet was told to call the wind "to breathe upon these slain, that they may live"—that they may undergo a spiritual revival, as well.

Likewise Judah Halevy, who can hardly be accused of being more concerned about the physical survival of the Jews than about Judaism, proclaimed that Prophecy can come into its own again only after the Jewish nation has returned to its land. He, too, realised that physical revival is an essential precondition for spiritual revival.

In this context reference should also be made to the greatest rabbinical figure of our times, the late Rabbi Abraham Hacohen Kook, undoubtedly as orthodox as any. His philosophy did not admit of any place in the world, including the secular, material world, as being devoid of some degree of godliness and sanctity. Still less so anything done for the sake of *Eretz Israel* and the Return to Zion, even if the doers are Jewish pioneers who fail to practise their religion. All material actions performed in *Eretz Israel* and on behalf of *Eretz Israel* assume a higher degree of sanctity, for they are done in a sacred cause and undoubtedly prepare the ground for the forthcoming spiritual renewal.

This spiritual revival will undoubtedly be the supreme stage of that miracle we are now witnessing: the renewal of

Jewish statehood in *Eretz Israel*. Like anything else in this transformation, it will undoubtedly not come about quietly and peacefully. Its birthpangs will be no less painful than those that any great revolution has to undergo. Much that is old and obsolete will have to be discarded, as our Prophets have repeatedly urged us to do. The fundamental spiritual values of our ancient faith will be reaffirmed in all their truth, in the light of which those pseudo-values imported from seventy countries and cultures of the diaspora will melt away into nothingness, and many of the foreign idols we still worship will tumble.

We are living in an era of fast-disintegrating concepts. Again, it is no accident that our return to *Eretz Israel* is taking place at a time when the hitherto dominant European civilisation is on the decline, having burnt itself out. We are located right at the meeting point between a waning Europe and a nascent Asia. We occupy this position not merely as go-betweens, but so that from our own ancient roots that have preserved their sap for two thousand years, and from which, being ours, we cannot and should not cut ourselves off, we may reconstitute and create anew.

No one can predict the form the resulting spiritual renascence will assume. It is clear, however, that it cannot materialise in the abstract, divorced from our territorial, national and political revival. Nor can it take place within a lilliputian country and a midget state. It requires a strong physical base, constituted by the majority of our nation and our potential, re-gathered in this country where we first became creative, and where nothing has ever been produced by any people except us. The renascence of the Jewish nation, the renascence of the land of the Jews, and the renascence of the Jewish spirit are thus of necessity conjoined and superimposed.

The attempts to escape the Jewish fate are behind us. So are the attempts to abjure *Eretz Israel,* in whole or in part. And in the depth of the Jewish people and its land, consciously or unconsciously, the first buds of a spiritual renascence are showing. Its time will come after the generations of the sons of Yiftah and Samson and David will have come and gone, and having done their duty, there will no longer be Jews in the diaspora struggling for their very existence. Thus there are three points of no return that, like the stages of our renascence, are closely interlinked. There can be no withdrawal from *Eretz Israel* because there is no going back on Zionism. And there is no going back on Zionism because there is no escape and retreat from Judaism.

By Judaism we do not mean that anemic travesty of our creed that was evolved during the Emancipation, when such Christian concepts as proffering the other cheek, and showing forgiveness to one's enemies were jumbled together into a kind of abstract Judaism divorced from the life and spirit of the people, and having no basis in the Law of Moses, in Prophecy or in sound Talmudic Judaism. The idea of redemption was voided of its Jewish, Scriptural and Talmudic contents and converted into an ephemeral Christian-individual concept having nothing to do with the Return to Zion, the ingathering of the exiles, the revival of the Kingdom of David and the recovery of the Promised Land. Needless to say, the everyday observance of the commandments was abandoned. In the flight from Jewish nationhood and in the craving for acceptance and conformism, a Mosaic religion was evolved that had little to do either with Moses or with religion. While Luther's reform was revolutionary, nonconformistic, and profoundly nationalistic, all our reform movements until shortly before establishment of the State of Israel were ultra-conformistic and anti-nationalistic, aiming at an easy-going, bloodless Judaism.

In Zionism, too, similar counter-revolutionary attempts were made by Achad Ha'am and Martin Buber to emasculate it and rob it of its healthy and health-giving elements —its territorial, national, if necessary military but certainly militant character. All these attempts at spiritualising either

Zionism or Judaism implied both de-Zionisation and de-Judaization. They were a defection from Jewish life and Jewish reality.

Events in Europe and in this country, the rise of Hitler and of Stalin, of Englishmen like Bevin and of Arabs such as Nasser, Hussein and Arafat worked on Zionism like a cold shower and restored its physical and mental health. Judaism, too, is gradually recovering its original vigour and is returning to its Biblical origins of Joshua and David—the conqueror of the land, and the composer of the psalms. For again, there can be no retreat from Davidic *Eretz Israel* just as there can be no retreat from Herzl's and Jabotinsky's Zionism and from full-blooded renascent Judaism.

History has shown that escape from all three is barred. And were it possible, would it be worthwhile? Is it not much better to yield to this necessity, which does not happen to be the worst of compulsions? If it is one of Sartre's existentialist *nuit clos,* or no-exit situations, is it not preferable to arrive at it by our own free choice than to have it rammed down our throats in the kind of hell in which Sartre's heroes are hopelessly trapped?

Why should we be forced by our enemies to liberate Jerusalem and *Eretz Israel?* Do they not deserve to be liberated by us as an act of our sovereign will? And why should only he whom the gentiles decree to be such, be a Jew, instead of his being a Jew proudly and of his own free will?

And in Zionist terms: Why come to Eretz Israel as a persecuted refugee rather than as a voluntary immigrant, an *oleh,* the Hebrew connotation of which is "one who ascends," in line with the concluding verse of the Bible, in its original sequence: "Whoever is among you of all his people, may the Lord his God be with him. Let him *go up.*" It is a two-fold ascension that connotes return to the homeland and to God.

15

ISRAEL

IN the controversy about territorial withdrawal in exchange for peace, the advocates of this course ask among other things, "Why do we need another million Arabs in a Jewish State of Israel?"

We shall not go into the kind of peace that can be expected in exchange for territorial concessions. Only people totally ignorant of Middle Eastern history, who have never heard of or read about the Arab states' true intentions as manifested over the years and who have forgotten what happened in 1948 and in 1967, when these states, respected members of the U.N. and its Security Council launched wars of extermination against us, besides their flaunting of the numerous international conventions guaranteeing the freedom of the seas, territorial integrity and so on—only such people can still wonder why Israel has little confidence in a peace treaty signed by the leaders of these states; especially a peace treaty under the terms of which decisive strategic areas revert into their hands. We, however, have learned to gauge the true value of such contracts, treaties, resolutions and conventions. At the first opportunity the Arabs will renege and try to expel us from this land. And we will go clamouring and pleading to the United Nations, as is our wont.

Our own experience and the experience of Vietnam have shown us that we must not allow a situation to develop where the Americans would feel constrained—as could happen—to send their own sons here to rescue us. We do not want their help, nor do we need it as long as we are left within the present boundaries which are the best guarantee for our safety.

But should we be forced to retreat, our existence will once again be threatened, a menace that implies the engulfment of the entire Middle East by the Russians. They will gradually swallow it by the notorious salami method—slice after slice. At best, the U.S.A. will have to come to our assistance not with arms alone but with men as well. American youngsters who are now reluctant to fight in the Far East will be called upon to fight in the Middle East.

Thus the present borders, essential for the survival of the State of Israel and the Jewish people, in the long run also prevent the Sovietization of the Middle East. Once firmly ensconced here, the Soviets will have a stranglehold over the whole of Asia, from where they will send out their tentacles into Africa and the European countries along the shores of the Mediterranean. Ultimately, our present borders thus also protect the life of many an American soldier.

Israel is the only force that can halt the Soviet advance —provided she holds on to the present territories at least. Though in this way peace cannot, perhaps, be restored tomorrow, but only the day after, nevertheless withdrawal entails the certainty of war not the day after tomorrow, but tomorrow.

To come back to the so-called demographic argument. Paradoxically it is advanced most frequently by "progressive" circles who have turned racist all of a sudden, and cannot tolerate a large Arab minority in the State of Israel, while the "reactionary" elements are quite willing to live side by side with it.

All that we are trying to do and achieve here, including the building of the Jewish city of Tel Aviv, is based on the Zionist idea that this state and this country are not designed solely for the Jews already living in them, but for those millions who are yet to come. With their arrival—and come they will, whether of their own volition or that of others—

the Arab minority will dwindle in proportion even if the more extreme but more humanitarian solution offered here for their organised mass transfer is not implemented.

As Itzhak Tabenkin, one of the foremost leaders of the leftist kibbutz movement, who is nevertheless firmly opposed to any withdrawal, has put it, "When you have a headache, do you go and cut your head off?" A big Arab minority may be a serious headache, but are a million Arabs outside the boundaries of the State of Israel any better for us, security-wise, than a million Arabs who are under our control? And in order to get rid of the headache they might cause us, are we to abandon this our land, the head and heart of the Jewish people?

So far the Arab minority has caused us no headaches because we know how to handle it with efficiency and respect. It has caused us far less trouble than did the Negroes to America or the Irish Catholics to the North of Ireland. For the last four years we have been living within the expanded territories that contain a million and a quarter Arabs, without experiencing any major headaches as a result. On the contrary, this new population has been undergoing a remarkable economic development and the new territories are being gradually integrated within the Israeli economy.

The main consideration, however, must be that a price has to be paid for the accomplishment of any ideal, the attainment of any privilege or liberty. Is Zionism not worth it all? Is, then, the Arab minority our sole source of trouble? It is only in a disintegrating society that side issues become dominant and combine to bring about its final dissolution. Israeli society, being both Jewish and Zionist and therefore highly dynamic, has always, thanks to its intrinsic mobility and pliability, been able to overcome the various strains and stresses exerted upon it.

Every liberation movement is bound to encounter a variety of problems. One has but to look at what is going on in Africa as a result of the liberation of this continent and the often far-too-rapid transition from a tribal, jungle culture to modern civilisation, straight from the tree to the jet without the intermediate stage of carriages and cars, and from fetishism to atheism without the intermediate monotheistic stage, frequently in a turmoil of tribal warfare. Does this cause anyone, especially anyone who considers himself progressive, to scrap the process of liberation because it involves too much headache and heartbreak? Does any serious-minded person—and I am not referring to a few individual desperadoes and deserters from society—suggest that humanity as a whole should step off the road of history and civilisation and go back to the jungle in line with Rousseau's sentimental preachings? The impossibility of such a sidetracking maneuver is obvious, beyond the cruel fact that the jungle happens to be far from idyllic. Nature is no paradise.

Similarly the Jewish liberation movement in *Eretz Israel*, born of so great and beautiful an ideal and filling such an essential need, is not something to be lightly given up. It must be served and pursued right to its goal, whatever the headaches and the heartbreaks and the suffering. For many it is no easy matter to wrench themselves away from accepted forms of life and thought, to be uprooted from familiar surroundings where the language, culture and economic structure are so totally different from that required here and now in *Eretz Israel*.

Zionism is leading the Jewish nation out of the hell of the diaspora—and by hell we do not mean only physical suffering but also moral and spiritual evil, the very idea of exile being evil whatever heavenly, material comforts it may offer. It does, however, make no pretence of leading straight through the gates of paradise. At one time, fortunately past, Zionism too had its romantic period, when both the ideal and its accomplishment were conceived of in idyllic terms. Quite apart from the question whether man is constituted to live in a goody-goody fairyland, the hard fact is that no such land is waiting around the corner—and no cause can be achieved in blissful felicity. Birthpangs, though they might be attenuated, are still a normal accompaniment of birth, yet it is somewhat abnormal for a woman to refuse to have children because of them.

The labour of Israel's rebirth is hard indeed, and the bleeding is heavy, though undoubtedly less than would have been the blood spilt if the conception had never taken place.

The State of Israel has many problems to contend with, and will have many more. There are the hot, desert winds, the *chamsin,* and there is a shortage of water. At the time of the first exodus, Moses promised our forefathers a land flowing with milk and honey; but those who took this land from us and inhabited it in the interim managed to wring it dry through their neglect and despoliation. When we first came back to it there was neither milk nor honey nor bread, nor meat nor fruit to feed the inhabitants. Now again it produces all these, thanks to our efforts born of our need. It is again coming close to what it was in ancient days: a land of citrus and avocado, of diamonds and planes—apart from milk and honey.

Just as the land, though it did indeed wait for us, did not remain in its primordial state, flowing with milk and honey, so the nation returning here is not made of pure gold. Some of the early immigrants, who came as pioneers driven by sheer idealism, constituted an elite both by virtue of their devotion and the cause to which they were dedicated. But *Eretz Israel* and Zionism were not designed solely for the chosen few, although certain wayward spirits like Achad Ha'am may have claimed so. The kibbutz might be an idyllic and ideal social structure, but in the perspective of history it served to break the ground, to undertake the hardest pioneering tasks of reclaiming barren soil or manning remote and dangerous border outposts. It was not a purpose in itself. The goal was to bring here millions of Jews of every type and variety.

The nation that Moses led out of Egypt also had its dross.

Far from being all righteous there were those who hankered after the fleshpots, worshipped the golden calf, were eternally dissatisfied, slandered the promised land and wanted to return to the exile of Egypt. There were tribal communities inflicted with a sense of inferiority and discrimination, and hippies whoring with Midianite temple prostitutes. Moses however, could take it easy and wander in the desert for forty years until the rabble might die off and a new generation arise. We have to turn a desert country and what many consider a desert people into a fruitful land and nation, without having the option of wandering forty years in the wilderness.

Not only are we denied this option, but instead of twelve tribes we have seventy-seven diasporas to deal with, from India to Ethiopia, from San Francisco to the Atlas mountains. On coming here they have no common language except the language of prayer, restored to everyday use. Their style of life ranges from the ultra-sophisticated to the primitive. Besides men of superior intellect there are illiterates and morons, religious believers and Communists, both divided into countless sub-sects, each convinced of having an exclusive hold on the truth.

We have problems of immigration and integration the like of which no other nation has ever had to contend with. Though the population has almost quadrupled in only two decades, constant efforts are being made to increase the flow. We look forward to the arrival of many more millions, even in one great wave, knowing full well the troubles and difficulties involved.

Thus, we have problems of climate and of water, of ethnic incompatibilities and differences in life-styles and standards of living. We have our religious problems, and our public administration leaves much to be desired because for two thousand years we have never run a state of our own, subsisting solely in a religious communal setting. All these problems, moreover, have to be tackled at a time of incessant external hostilities, and sometimes in a state of virtual international isolation—after being debilitated by the great Nazi slaughter that deprived us of valuable Jewish, Zionist and human resources.

Often one can only stand and wonder how, in spite of all these apparently insurmountable obstacles so much has been and is being done. Religious Jews would ascribe it to an act of Divine will, of the immanent godhead that was, is and shall be, as his Hebrew name implies. But even nonbelievers cannot regard this as an ordinary liberation movement running its normal course. They too must admit that this is a unique historical phenomenon. We are witnessing the revival of our nonconformist character and strength, and this time not as religious rebels smashing heathen idols nor as stubborn survivors in an environment that hates us and wants to engulf us by assimilation, nor as individual revolutionaries fighting an obsolete capitalist society, but as a national collective that is re-uniting after dispersion. After generations of centrifugal motion, the Jewish people has reversed its course: Thanks to the force generated by its new centripetal motion, it is able to overcome the counter-pull of many material and spiritual as well as political and demographic forces, surmounting geographic obstacles as well as its own weaknesses, to create a new Hebrew culture in an ancient land and from ancient sources.

The sacrifice required of us by way of individual liberties and material comforts is small compared with the greatness of the revolution that we are making, and even the loss of life and limb, however heavy, does not measure up to its magnitude. The Jews who have come from Islamic countries have been liberated, in a very material sense, from the dire poverty and shameful segregation to which they were subject. The Jews from Communist countries are liberated from a tyrannical dictatorship. For the Jews of the West who so far are suffering neither material want nor political oppression, *Eretz Israel* holds out the means to leave before it is too late, before events similar to those that happened in Europe recur in greater or lesser intensity. In a period of rapid change, what may seem a remote eventuality can come about with unexpected precipitancy, and who can tell what may happen five or twenty years hence?

In all respects, from the physical, material, ethical and spiritual point of view, *Eretz Israel* has much to offer to the Jew as an individual. Nevertheless, Zionism no longer holds out utopian promises, which inevitably culminate in disappointment and recrimination. The facts as they are should be depicted in their true light. Before a lasting peace can be achieved, there may still be battles and wars. We are suffering from excessive bureaucratization and unnecessary party politics. For the religious Jew there is much that goes against his sense of decorum and piety. Paradoxically, for the secular Jew there are many problems, especially relating to matters of personal status, that are bound up with the peculiar Jewish symbiosis of nationality and religion. For many generations religion has been our main source of cultural expression, and any disruption of this bond may lead to serious divisions. There also are many social injustices that are an inevitable outcome of the rapid population increase. All these are problems which, had it not been for the essential, major problem would cause an outcry and endless trouble.

For is there any country in the world that is free from problems? And above all, is it not worthwhile for the sake of a great cause like ours, to try and find intermediate solutions or even to stave off some ancilliary problems? It was no accident that after the Six Day War all ethnic tensions ceased; when the Moroccan and Iraqi Jews, for example, realised that on the field of battle all Jews are equal, and that there was no truth in the false allegation spread by hostile elements that they, the "Arab" Jews, were being used as cannon fodder. Common ideas and dangers are a uniting force. They breed a spirit of competition not in the pursuit of material comforts, but in the interest of the cause, in devotion and self-sacrifice.

We still have created no paradise here. Sometimes it smacks somewhat more of hell. But it is our hell, and our job to turn it into the paradise we want, a task which we have every prospect of accomplishing. Drawing up the overall account, everything was and is worthwhile, also from the materialistic, individual point of view, although for the time being the account must be made in terms of the collective and the cause.

The miracle is being achieved by rational and irrational forces, through the willing sacrifice of pioneers and the dire distress of Jewish existence. Heaven and earth, as the ancient Hebrew idiom has it, have combined to perform the miracle of Israel and *Eretz Israel*. It is not a return to a lost garden of Eden, which might not be so pleasurable even if it were possible. On the contrary, the Return to Zion is proceeding in full knowledge of all the difficulties and troubles involved —external and internal, old and new, local and general, material and moral, public and individual. But above all there is the guiding awareness of the central problem, the highest challenge: the salvation of the Jewish people in its homeland. This is the supreme personal, national and human challenge. What has been accomplished so far in meeting it is unequalled in its beauty and greatness, in its need-and-wish fulfilment. What may yet be done in the future is hard to imagine.

In every perspective, the metaphysical and the historical as well as the psychological and individual, it is a challenge that must be met in spite of all problems, and perhaps precisely because of them. It is essential for the sake of our human image, created as we were in the image of God, that we take up this challenge and face it squarely.

By doing so we are again ascending the existential philosophical ladder that appeared to our forefather Jacob —the most dynamic of the three—on his flight from Esau: A ladder placed on the earth, its top reaching into heaven, and angels going up and down—whether on the ladder or on the dreamer, the text does not say.

For many years this our ladder was hanging in heaven and our angels were moving on the upper rungs, flapping in the wind. We were in some way schizophrenic, hypermaterialistic and hyperspiritualistic at one and the same time. Now we are again placing our ladder firmly on the ground. But we are not giving up its heavenly dimension which is deep inside us, in our blood. Nor shall we give up those ethical, humane, idealistic angels which are likewise part of our flesh. They will, however, no longer be swinging free without ground under their feet. For as long as there is no soil, no land, no real security and material life, there is no real existence for the ladder that symbolises our essence.

It was when Jacob came back to *Eretz Israel* from his first exile, after his flight—and he had the good sense to come back loaded with property before he had been robbed of it—that he fought with men and with God (Gen. 32, 28); his victory earned him the proud name:

ISRAEL

Times of Israel

Cover Reproductions

Issue No. 1/009

"... and I will make of thee a great nation."
(Exodus)

Issue No. 1/011

LET MY PEOPLE GO
Cover painted in Israel by Yosif Kuzkovsky. Born in Russia 1902, escaped from Russia 1969. Died Tel Aviv 1970.

ISRAEL AND THE

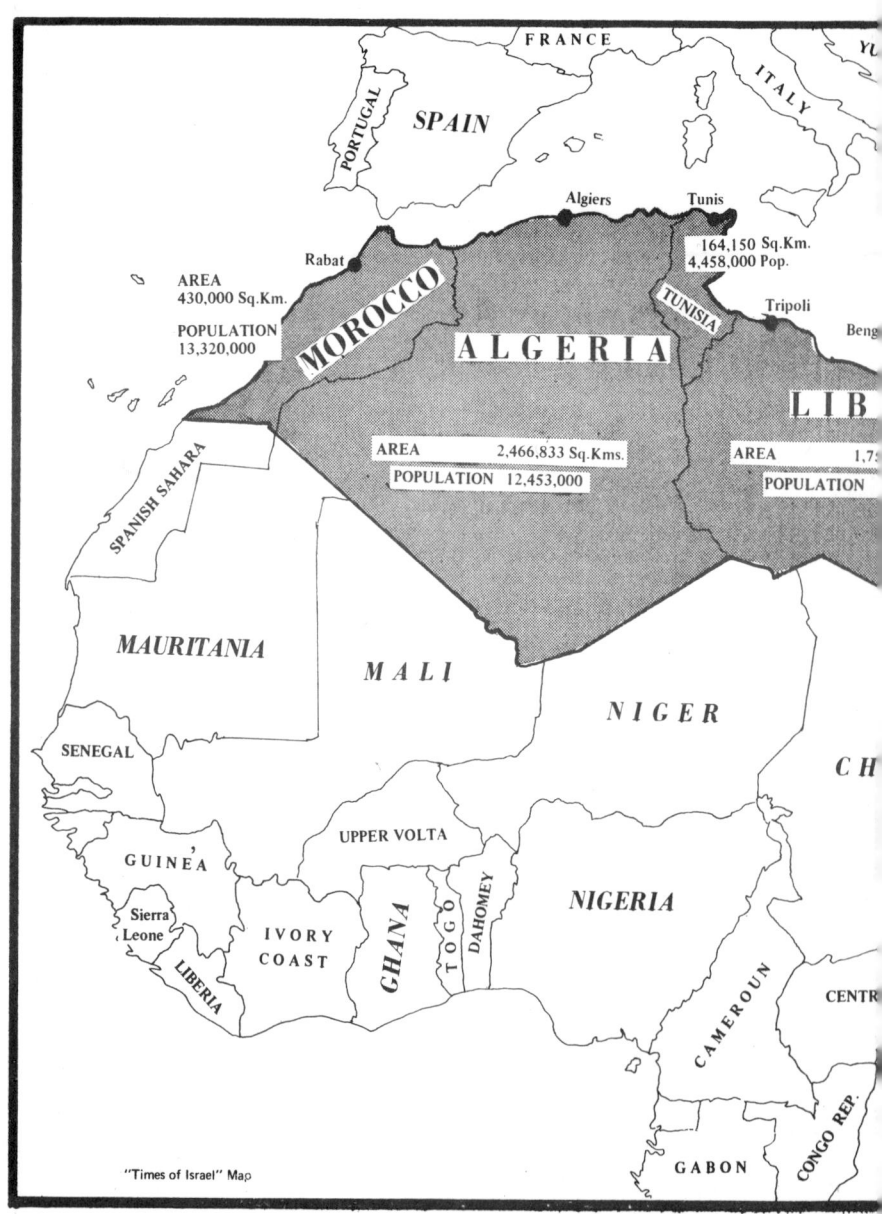

"Times of Israel" Map